FROM THE PEN OF PAUL

THE FANTASTIC IMAGES OF

FROM THE PEN OF PAUL
THE FANTASTIC IMAGES OF
FRANK R. PAUL

edited and with an introduction by
STEPHEN D. KORSHAK

preface by
SIR ARTHUR C. CLARKE, K.B.E.

special contribution by
JERRY WEIST & ROGER HILL

SHASTA-PHOENIX
Books of Lasting Significance
Orlando, Florida

In Memory of
Sir Arthur C. Clarke and Forrest J Ackerman

The collective work, *From the Pen of Paul: Fantastic Images of Frank R. Paul*,
is © Shasta-Phoenix Publishers 2009. All Rights Reserved.

Introduction copyright © 2009 by **Stephen D. Korshak**
Preface copyright © 2009 by **Stephen D. Korshak**
Frank R. Paul: Illustrator to Tomorrow's Visions copyright © 2009 by **Jerry Weist** and **Roger Hill**
Bibliography copyright © 2009 by **Frank Wu**
Bibliographical Index for the Science-Fiction Artwork of Frank R. Paul
copyright © 2009 by **Jerry Weist** and **Robert Weinberg**

Publisher: **Erle Melvin Korshak**
Editor: **Stephen D. Korshak**
Art Direction: **Robert V. Conte**
Consulting Editor and Art Director: **J. David Spurlock**

Cover designed by **Mark McNabb**, **Patricia Fabricant** and **Robert V. Conte**
Layout and Production by **Bob Fillie** and **Patricia Fabricant** for **Chikara Entertainment, Inc.**

Special thanks are due to the following for permission to reproduce in this volume Frank R. Paul artwork from their collections:
Glynn Crain, Douglas Ellis, the Howard and Jane Frank Collection, Eric Gewirz, James Halperin, Dr. Christine Haycock, the Erle Melvin Korshak and Stephen Dedalus Korshak Collection, Robert Lesser, the Family of Frank R. Paul, Robert Weinberg, and **Jerry Weist.**

Special thanks to **Jerry Weist** for the images to most Pulp covers, and for writing
the majority of captions on artwork and periodicals.

Additional thanks to **Ian Weist** and **Roberta Jarvis** for their technical assistance, and **John Gunnison** at Adventure House.

For information, address the publisher:
Shasta/Phoenix Publishers, 8680 Commodity Circle, Suite 200B, Orlando, FL 32819

Library of Congress Cataloging-in-Publication Data
From The Pen of Paul: The Fantastic Images of Frank R. Paul,
edited by Stephen D. Korshak.
Includes bibliographic references.
1. Paul, Frank R.,Themes, motives. 2. Science fiction–Illustration.
I. Paul, Frank R., 1884–1963. II. Korshak, Stephen D. 1952–

ISBN 978-0-9800931-3-1 (Ultra Deluxe edition) - $395.00
ISBN 978-0-9800931-2-4 (Deluxe edition) - $59.95
ISBN 978-0-9800931-1-7 (Hardcover edition) - $39.95
ISBN 978-0-9800931-0-0 (Softcover edition) - $24.95

First Printing, May 2009

www.shasta-phoenix.com

Printed in China

Frontispiece: From the collection of Robert Lesser. *Amazing Stories Magazine* back cover.

Dedicated to

SAM MOSKOWITZ

My mentor in this volume

and my longtime friend.

—Stephen D. Korshak

Photograph courtesy of the Sam Moskowitz collection. Digitally enhanced by Marc McNabb.

CONTENTS

* Featured only in the Deluxe and Ultra Deluxe Editions of this book.

November · WRNY · 25 Cents
IN CANADA—THIRTY CENTS

AMAZING STORIES

HUGO GERNSBACK
EDITOR

Scientifiction

Stories by
David H. Keller, M.D.
Walter Kateley
B. and Geo. C. Wallis

PAUL

HOMAGE TO PAUL

preface by
SIR ARTHUR C. CLARKE, K.B.E.

The very first science-fiction magazine I ever saw had a cover by Frank Paul—and it is one of the most remarkable illustrations in the history of science fiction, as it appears to be a clear example of precognition on the part of the artist!

I must have seen *Amazing Stories* for November 1928 about a year after it had been shipped across to England—so rumor has it, as ship's "ballast"—and sold at Woolworth's for 3p. How I used to haunt that once-famous store during my lunch hour, in search of issues of *Amazing*, *Wonder* and *Astounding*, buried like jewels in the junk-pile of detective and western pulps!

The painting shows a tropical beach, complete with palm trees, on which a spaceship looking like a farm silo with picture windows has just descended. Five explorers have emerged and are gazing in astonishment—as well they might—at the enormous bulk of Jupiter dominating the sky. The Great Red Spot is staring back at them like a baleful eye, and an inner moon is in transit.

But the most extraordinary thing about the painting is that it shows details of turbulence in the equatorial belt which, I feel reasonably certain, were not known to exist until the Voyager missions almost half a century later. Did Paul have access to telescope drawings which hinted at these details? I have never seen any such myself; perhaps an expert on Jupiter can resolve the mystery....

Quite apart from this, that November *Amazing Stories* cover is one of the all-time classics of science-fiction art. To my mind, Paul remains the undisputed king of the pulp artists—his covers were colorful, imaginative, and intelligent. And although his human beings all appeared cast from the same mould, his range of aliens was unmatched. I can still recall the crowded street in "The City of Singing Flame," even though I have not seen it for half a century. It makes the famous bar scene in *Star Wars* look like a meeting of the local Republican Committee—and incidentally, proves that Paul was as much a master of black and white as of colour.

Lesser-known examples of Paul's work also appeared in the yearly Christmas cards which Hugo Gernsback sent out, showing improbable inventions, and often making fun of his own ideas. I received these from Hugo for many years—they must be quite valuable now, and I am sorry that mine have now been lost. (I think—unless they turn up some day in the Clarkives.)

I only once had the privilege of meeting Paul, at a World Science Fiction Convention in New York, which must have been around 1960. I was so over-awed that I remember very little of the encounter, but still recall the incident with affection and gratitude, as I felt I was talking to a gentle and cultured man.

ARTHUR C. CLARKE
Colombo, Sri Lanka

Sir Arthur wrote this homage prior to his death on March 18, 2008.

Opposite: AMAZING STORIES pulp cover, November 1928.

IN SEARCH OF FRANK R. PAUL

introduction by
STEPHEN D. KORSHAK

He was a simple man, unpretentious, not given to hyperbole or self-promotion, and his vital statistics are sparse indeed. Born in 1884 in the Imperial City of Vienna during the declining years of Hapsburg rule, Paul's family wanted him to dedicate his life to the priesthood. He willed it otherwise. Instead, he studied art in Vienna and then in Paris and then in London, where he completed special courses in architectural and mechanical drafting, and the impact of these courses is evident in his brilliant and original science-fiction artwork.

He arrived in New York in 1906 at the age of 22 and found work as a political cartoonist at the Jersey City *Jersey Journal.* In 1914 he met Hugo Gernsback, himself a German-speaking immigrant, and began illustrating for Gernsback's early publications: *Electrical Experimenter, Modern Electrics,* and *Science and Invention* wherein appeared from time to time some early science fiction. By 1926, when Gernsback's *Amazing Stories* was born, Paul was ready: a talented calligrapher, Paul not only created the magazine's famed comet logo, but also the front cover painting and all of the interior black and white illustrations. Subsequently, over the span of his career, he was to paint over 200 published covers and in excess of 1,000 black and white interiors.

In addition to magazine illustration, Paul was responsible for the design of dozens of buildings in New York City and environs, the most famous of which was the Johnson & Johnson building in New Brunswick, New Jersey, hailed in 1938 as the single most outstanding example of industrial architecture in the United States.

Married in 1913, at the time of his death in 1963 he had been married 50 years and left besides his widow three daughters and a son.

So much for the public man. But what about the private man, this individual human being?

That Paul was generous of his time and of himself is legendary. In the Fall of 1939 my father, Erle Melvin Korshak—destined within a decade to become one of the pre-eminent pioneers of science-fiction book publishing—was living in Manhattan and

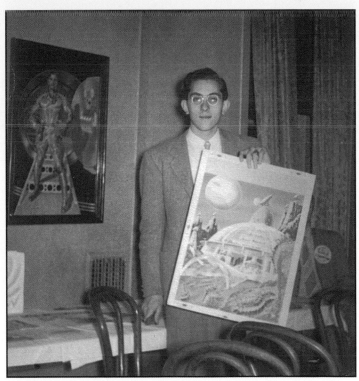

Above: Shasta publisher, Erle Melvin Korshak, auctioneering the original Frank R. Paul back cover illustration shown on the opposite page, and sold at the second World Science Fiction Convention in Chicago in 1940.

Opposite: *Frank R. Paul,* original painting for "Glass City of Europa," gouache on board, signed by the artist. From the Korshak Collection.

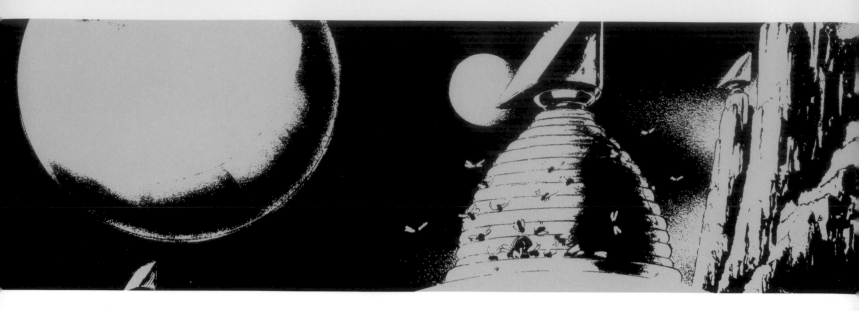

attending New York's famous Peter Stuyvesant High School, then at 15th street on the East side. Paul's office and studio were but a few blocks away on the opposite side of Union Square. And my father, an avid admirer of the artist, often stopped to say "hello" on his way home from school.

As the Holiday Season was fast approaching, my father, who then, like many of the early sci-fi fans, fancied himself an artist, had prepared a sketch of a Holiday card he planned to produce for his friends and family that year, and he wanted to show his efforts to his friend. Paul looked at my father's sketch and, without another word, created then and there a simple but vastly superior rendition of the scene my father had shown him. With a flourish Paul presented it to my father as a gift and, of course, my father ecstatically had it reproduced.

In the Paul archive assembled by Sam Moskowitz which his widow, Dr. Christine Haycock, sent to me for the purpose of this book, I came across a letter to the editor of the *Bergen Evening Record* written six years before his death.

I commend this letter, in its entirety, to everyone who reads this book.

Stephen D. Korshak in front of the Frank R. Paul back cover he acquired in 2000, 60 years after his father sold it at auction. Photo by John L. Coker, III.

July 16, 1957
Editor
Bergen Evening Journal
Hackensack, New Jersey

Dear Sir:

In your obituary article of May 13th of the late Mayor Blakeney of Rivervale you mention photographs of two paintings "owned" by Mr. Blakeney and descriptive of the Colonel Baylor massacre at Rivervale during the Revolutionary war, which were presented to the Pascack Historical Society. Since these paintings have some historical value, why were not the original color paintings turned over to the Society instead of more photographic copies?

You see, I am the man who painted these pictures at the height of the depression, not as a personal present for Mr. Blakeney, but as sketches submitted for murals in the Rivervale Municipal Building which was new at the time. I had hoped to paint the murals as a WPA project in order to get enough money to pay my taxes and interest on a mortgage, which would have saved my home and, at the same time, to show future generations the role Rivervale played in the War of Independence. Artists all over the country were helped in this way.

A great deal of research went into these pictures. --- But I might just as well have saved my time and effort, because nothing was ever done about helping me out of a financial squeeze.

Few people now will remember those dark days: the depression went on and on, work was non-existent, reserves eaten up, serious illness in my family, children in school, no money for lawyers when the law allowed a $7,000 mortgage to take a 25-acre improved property with brook running through it, standing timber, and a new ten room house on it.

I don't think anybody can blame me for coming to the conclusion that some of Colonel Bayler's Hessians of 1776 must have settled in Rivervale and Park Ridge, because these modern Hessians showed the same characteristic—always glad and ready to help a neighbor in trouble by a stab in the back.

After submitting these sketches to Mr. Blakeney for the purpose stated, I never received a word about them—not even an acknowledgement. Here, twenty years later, I find that he considered them his personal property. This is to keep the record straight.

Yours sincerely,
Frank R. Paul

"FRP/ph
Home address: 700 Cedar Lane · Teaneck, New Jersey
Frank R. Paul"

Res ipsa loquiter. The thing speaks for itself.

Stephen D. Korshak
Orlando, Florida

Frank R. Paul at his drawing board, circa 1950.
Photo courtesy of Joan C. Engle, © Copyright the family of Frank R. Paul.

FRANK R. PAUL: ILLUSTRATOR TO TOMORROW'S VISIONS

Special Contribution by

ROGER HILL & JERRY WEIST

His cover illustration caused a young Isaac Asimov to pick up the first science-fiction magazine he had ever seen, while working at the Asimov family candy store in New York City. The year was 1926. During the same year, on the other side of the country in San Francisco, another young boy, Forrest J Ackerman, picked up his first issue of *Amazing Stories* with its colorful cover by this same artist of aliens making first contact with a human being. Two years later in Somerset, England, a young Arthur C. Clarke purchased his first science-fiction magazine, enthralled by a magically painted depiction of the gas giant Jupiter as viewed from one of its moons. As Clarke would later note, the pristine details of Jupiter could not possibly have been recorded by any existing telescopes of the time, and yet in stark clarity here stood the planet in all its highly-detailed sense of wonder. Ray Bradbury remembers his first cover by this same artist being *Amazing Stories Quarterly* for the fall of 1928, with its fantastic rendering of a giant ant. For an entire generation of authors to come, and young painters still learning their craft, as well as the first great generation of science-fiction fans, this artist would forever define everything that was exciting and wonderful about the genre of the fantastic, and the beginnings of what we now call science-fiction. The artist's name was Frank R. Paul.

The name of Frank R. Paul may not be as recognizable today to the fans that collect and read mainstream science fiction, but his accomplishments in the field of imaginative fiction during the 1920s to the 1960s, will forever be enshrined in the memories of those who have come into contact with his work. Many years ago, organized science-fiction fandom recognized this talented gentleman as the Father of Science-Fiction Illustrators, and accordingly he was the Guest of

Frank R. Paul and Rudolpha Rigelsen circa 1913, shortly after their marriage. Photograph courtesy of Joan C. Engle, © Copyright the family of Frank R. Paul.

Above: Rudolpha Rigelsen, early days at Rivervale. Photo courtesy of Joan C. Engle, © Copyright the family of Frank R. Paul.

Below: *Frank R. Paul,* illustration for the April 1920 issue of the ELECTRICAL EXPERIMENTER. Hugo Gernsback is pictured at the top center and the artist has drawn himself in the upper left corner with pens sticking out of his hair.

Honor at the first World Science Fiction Convention held in New York in 1939.

Although Paul had strong interests and training in all forms of architecture, his specialty was in isometric drafting, which involves the converting of blueprints into three-dimensional objects, or illustrations. As a sideline, he became an illustrator of school and college textbooks on subjects including biology, chemistry, history and physics. He also did advertising illustrations on a freelance basis, working out of his studio office located at 71 Fifth Avenue in New York City.

As chance would have it, around 1914 he was introduced to Hugo Gernsback through an art agency that Paul was providing illustration work for. At the time, Gernsback was a publisher of scientific journals (and a pioneer in the young field of radio) who headed The Experimenter Publishing Company located down the street from Paul's offices at 230 Fifth Ave. The two men soon discovered they were both European immigrants and enjoyed common interests in factual, modern science, invention, and technology. Gernsback was so taken with Paul's talents that he quickly hired the artist to become a regular freelance contributor to his magazines *Modern Electrics* and *Electrical Experimenter.* By 1920, this later title was changed to *Electrical Experimenter: Science and Invention,* and then eventually *Science and Invention.*

During the 1920s, Gernsback's science magazines featured cover artwork by the accomplished artist Howard V. Brown, who would paint many of the scientifiction theme covers, while Paul did the interior illustrations for these same issues. Brown was responsible for the striking cover art for the August 1923 issue of *Science and Invention* entitled Scientific Fiction Number. This issue is generally considered to be the first prototype science-fiction magazine, predating the debut of *Amazing Stories* by almost

GERNSBACK'S EDUCATIONAL LIBRARY №1

**HOW TO BUILD
4 DOERLE
SHORT WAVE SETS**

10 CENTS

*EVERYTHING
about ALL
the famous
DOERLE
RECEIVERS*

RADIO PUBLICATIONS, 101 HUDSON ST., NEW YORK CITY

GERNSBACK'S EDUCATIONAL LIBRARY. №2

**HOW TO MAKE THE
MOST POPULAR
ALL WAVE
1 and 2 TUBE RECEIVERS**

10 CENTS

RADIO PUBLICATIONS,
101 HUDSON ST.,
NEW YORK CITY

**A.C.
AND BATTERY
LOUDSPEAKER
SETS**

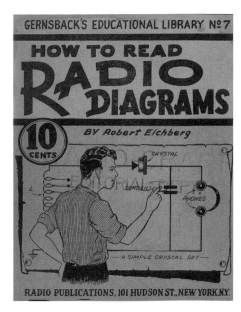

GERNSBACK'S EDUCATIONAL LIBRARY №7

**HOW TO READ
RADIO DIAGRAMS**

BY Robert Eichberg

10 CENTS

CRYSTAL

PHONES

— A SIMPLE CRYSTAL SET —

RADIO PUBLICATIONS, 101 HUDSON ST., NEW YORK, N.Y.

three years. Paul did the interior illustrations for this important publication, including works for G. Peyton Wertenbaker's "The Man From the Atom," and "Around the Universe," by Ray Cummings. He also prepared numerous covers and interior drawings for various Gernsback How-To booklets dealing mostly with television and radio—both being subjects the publisher had great interest in promoting. The most famous of these publications was the summer 1927 one-shot entitled *All About Television,* which featured a Frank R. Paul cover painting depicting the scene of a family in the future watching a football game on their living room television!

For the next fifteen years he would prove to be a most prolific artist, providing hundreds of technical pen and ink illustrations, using both a straight pen-line and an ink-wash or ink-splatter approach for the various scientific theories and subjects of modern technology he was assigned. As he developed and matured, he also became a master of calligraphy while hand-lettering titles for the stories he illustrated. Paul's clean linework and precise illustrative abilities would soon become a trademark of all Gernsback publications.

In early 1926 (nearly three years after his groundbreaking one-shot August 1923 issue of

Above: *Frank R. Paul,* "How to Build Dorle Short Wave Sets," *Gernsback's Educational Library No. 1,* Radio Publications, with Numbers 2 and 7.

Left: *Frank R. Paul,* illustration for "Doctor Hackensaw's Secrets" by Celment Fezandie. From a series of fictional stories run in continuing issues of SCIENCE AND INVENTION. This illustration ran in the September 1923 issue.

Science and Invention), Gernsback asked Paul to design a logo for the first issue of a new magazine he was planning. When Paul finished the now-famous perspective comet-tailed logo design, he quickly sketched in a rough-illustration to help set off the overall appearance of the work. Before he could tighten up the drawing and finish it off, Gernsback snapped it up and hurried it off to the printer. Shortly thereafter, the first issue of *Amazing Stories,* dated April of 1926 and devoted totally to scientifiction, hit the newsstands of America. The cover depicted a scene from the first installment of a two-part story by Jules Verne inside titled "Off On a Comet." It would be the first of many covers Paul would turn out for *Amazing* during the next three years. It's interesting to note here that for almost every Gernsback cover painting that Paul rendered with paints, he also had to create a smaller version, rendered in black and white, with pen and ink. These were used for house ads to sell individual copies of Gernsback magazines and to entice readers to subscribe to the different publications.

As early as 1911, Gernsback—publisher, author, editor, and theorist—had experimented with writing and publishing short or serialized stories of a science-fiction nature for inclusion in his different scientific magazines. In fact, it was during this time period that he coined the phrase "scientifiction," later re-named "science-fiction" in his editorial for the first issue of *Science Wonder Quarterly* for June of 1929.

With his profound knowledge of architecture and an imagination to accompany it, Paul was able to combine these elements into creating realistic, believable shapes of things to come. He created majestic depictions of futuristic cities, intricate machinery, alien life forms and landscapes, prehistoric monsters, space travelers, rocket ships, robots and death rays of destruction, all of which set the backdrop for some of the most incredible stories ever published. Popular authors such as Edgar Rice Burroughs, David H. Keller, Otis Adelbert Kline, Edgar Allan Poe, Jules Verne, Jack Williamson and H. G. Wells were just a few of the talented writers Paul came to illustrate in the pages of *Amazing.* As the artist recalled years later in an

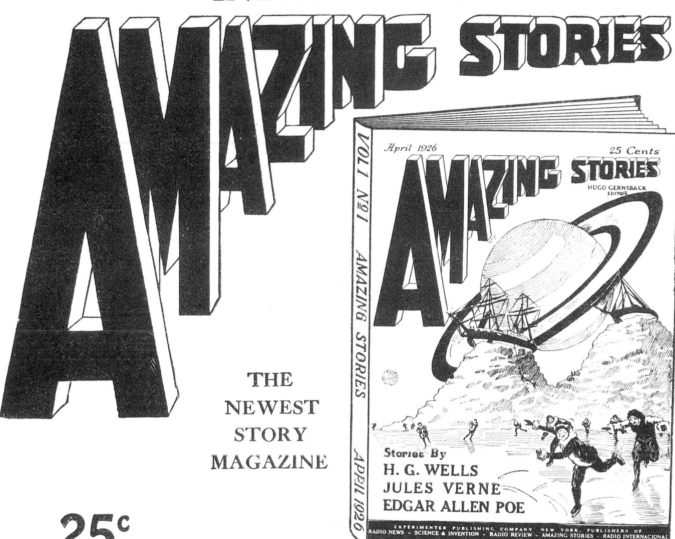

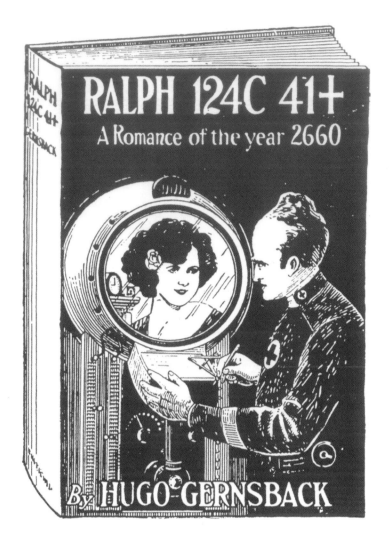

usually, required few corrections. I had been in the habit of outlining to Paul in a few short sentences practically all of my intricate projects and then watched him draw a rough sketch of any particular idea, often in less than ten minutes. We then went over the sketch while I made additional suggestions or modifications. Paul then executed the final drawings or painting. Curiously enough, many of these paintings were requested by Paul's fans and most of them are no longer in our possession."

Gernsback's comments about Paul's fans requesting his paintings were not overstated in the least. In fact, by late 1929 the demand was so great that Steller Publishing started running ads in the back pages of *Science Wonder,* offering full-color reproductions of the cover paintings (without logos or production paste-ons) for $1.00 each, postpaid. As described in one of the advertisements, on page 566 of the November issue, showing a photograph of a young lady holding Paul's *Science Wonder* covers, "These covers are exactly the same size as the artist's paintings (18" x 25") and made with the same 13 full colors that were used in making the original. Covers are made of heavy flexible mat board that makes them well deserving of a frame, a suitable picture to be hung in any home, classroom or clubhouse." As popular as Paul's paintings were at this time, very few of his original cover paintings from this early period have survived, and to this date science-fiction author and art historian Bob Weinberg has confirmed that not a single existing example of the Gernsback mat

Above: *Frank R. Paul,* original black and white design for Hugo Gernsback's RALPH 124C 41+, A Romance of the year 2660, from SCIENCE AND INVENTION 1920s advertising section.

Right: *Frank R. Paul,* logo design for The Science Fiction League, used on stationery, the club membership certificate card, and in ads in SCIENCE WONDER from 1929 through 1932.

Certificate of Membership

IS A MEMBER IN GOOD STANDING OF THE **SCIENCE FICTION LEAGUE** AND IS PLEDGED TO COOPERATE IN THE FURTHERANCE AND BETTERMENT OF SCIENCE FICTION.

THE EXECUTIVE BOARD

2001 NATIONAL CHAPTER 22 WEST 48th ST. NEW YORK CITY

SPONSORED BY THRILLING WONDER STORIES MAGAZINE

Frank R. Paul, original dust jacket design for Hugo Gernsback's RALPH 124C 41+, The Stratford Company, Boston, 1925.

Sam Moskowitz at home with three of the saved Frank R. Paul paintings from his tenure at SCIENCE FICTION PLUS. Photo courtesy of Christine Moskowitz.

Opposite, top: *Frank R. Paul,* illustration for QUIP MAGAZINE, Hugo Gernsback, December 25, 1949, this illustration from page 11. Photo courtesy of the collection of Jerry Weist.

Opposite, bottom: *Frank R. Paul,* cover illustration for FANTASY TIMES, No. 200, June 1954, James V. Taurasi publisher. Photo courtesy of the collection of Jerry Weist.

art for *Superworld Comics;* a short-lived science-fiction comic book published by Gernsback. Publishing under the name of Komos Publications, Gernsback managed to put out three issues of *SuperWorld* between April and August of 1940, before canceling the title. Paul contributed the cover and a feature for each issue, which was his last work associated with the comic-book field.

When science-fiction fandom began to organize during the mid 1930s, Paul's popularity was such that his original illustrations began showing up in auctions held at science-fiction conventions around the country. This previously unheard of opportunity to acquire Paul originals first took place at the 1st World Science Fiction Convention, held in New York City, over the Labor Day weekend of 1939. Originals continued to be offered at auction again in Chicago in 1940 and the following year at the Denvention (the 3rd World Science Fiction Convention) where Stanton Coblentz's "Into The Plutonian Depths," the cover for the spring 1931 *Wonder Stories Quarterly*, was auctioned off to a lucky attending fan. A rare photo still exists of Erle M. Korshak, publisher of this book (and the auctioneer at both Chicon I and Denvention) auctioning the Paul painting on page 11.

Because of the love of these early fans for Paul's work, and the efforts of many early convention attendees such as Forrest J Ackerman, David Kyle, Erle M. Korshak, Sam Moskowitz, and many others, the original paintings in this volume have been allowed to survive to this day intact. The most celebrated example of Paul's work being saved literally from the trash-bin was in 1953 when Sam Moskowitz, then editor for *Science-Fiction Plus* (with Gernsback as publisher) found that a janitor was leaving the building with several Paul paintings, headed for the trash! Sam stopped the man, and upon confirming with Gernsback that the paintings were indeed going to the dumpster, persuaded Gernsback to let him take them from the New York City offices to his home in New Jersey. Moskowitz would later enthrall his fellow fans at conventions with this story and complain that it was the most expensive "cab-fare" of his life!

As the 1940s rolled around, a boom in the science-fiction magazine market began to take place. Paul began receiving an increased demand for his work. New science-fiction titles were beginning to appear at a rapid pace and editors who had grown up reading the old *Amazing Stories* had great affection for Paul's art as did many of their readers. He was called upon to provide numerous pen and ink line drawings for Popular Publications' new reprint titles, *Famous Fantastic Mysteries* and *Fantastic Novels*. Both of these magazines featured reprints of many of the early classic "science-fantasy" type stories that had originally appeared in Munsey's *All Story Weekly* and *Argosy* magazines during the early 1900s. By this time Paul was very busy with other projects and considered his work for the science fiction magazine market a part-time job. The pay had never been that lucrative but he loved doing the work and stuck with it as much as possible. After Pearl Harbor, and with the United States thrown into a war against Japan and

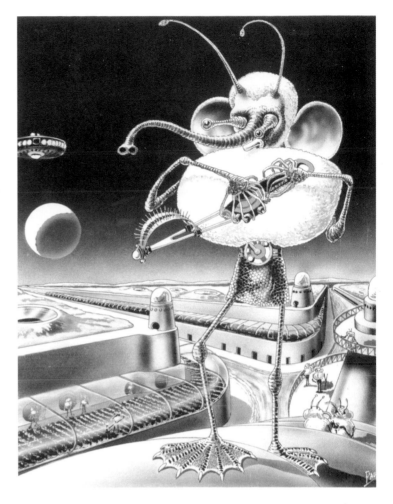

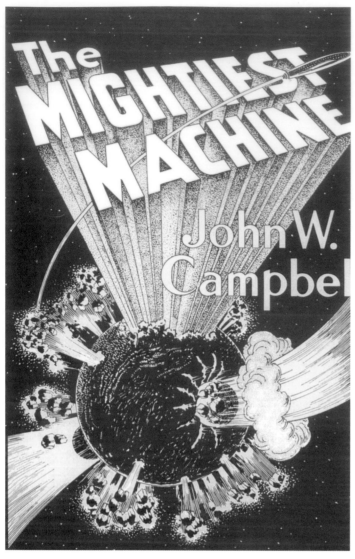

Above left: *Frank R. Paul,* cover illustration for John W. Campbell's THE MIGHTIEST MACHINE, Hadley Publishing Company, 1947.

Above right: *Frank R. Paul,* advertisement for Sam Moskowitz's THE IMMORTAL STORM, E.S.F.O. Press, Atlanta, 1954.

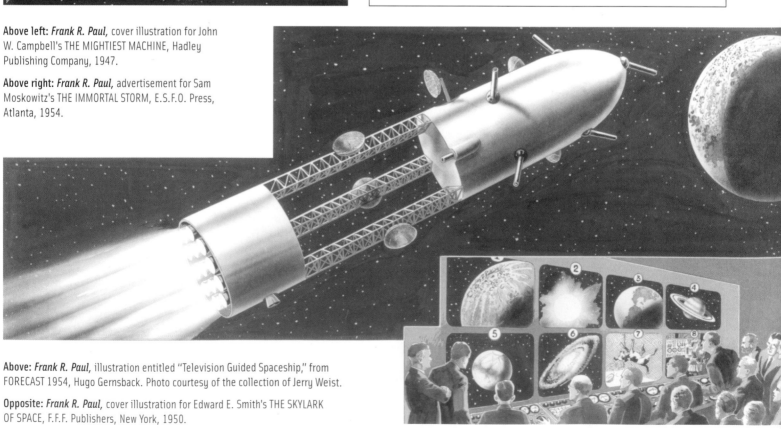

Above: *Frank R. Paul,* illustration entitled "Television Guided Spaceship," from FORECAST 1954, Hugo Gernsback. Photo courtesy of the collection of Jerry Weist.

Opposite: *Frank R. Paul,* cover illustration for Edward E. Smith's THE SKYLARK OF SPACE, F.F.F. Publishers, New York, 1950.

The Skylark of Space

by Edward E. Smith, Ph.D.

THE TALE OF THE FIRST INTER-STELLAR CRUISE

Germany, Paul had little time for science-fiction illustration. During the war years he was offered and accepted a salary doing design work for the government.

It's ironic that as prolific as Paul was in illustrating magazine covers and interior illustrations, this talent did not transfer into science-fiction book illustration. His only noted exceptions of science-fiction book covers are for Hugo Gernsback's 1925 novel *RALPH 124C 41+* (published by Stratford Company, Boston,) which featured the frontispiece also on the cover with eight additional black and white interior plates. In 1946 The Buffalo Book Company used one of Paul's illustrations from John Tain's *Wonder Stories* magazine illustration to *The Time Stream* for the hardcover dust jacket cover illustration. Paul also did the cover illustrations for John W. Campbell's *Mightiest Machine* (F.F.F. Publishers, Hadley Publishing, Providence, 1947), and Edward E. Smith's *Skylark of Space* (F.F.F. Publishers, Brooklyn, 1950). For each of these titles the artist rendered black and white illustrations used for the cover dust jackets. *The Complete Book of Outer Space* issued by Gnome Press in 1953 featured work by Paul as did *The Immortal Storm,* written by famed science-fiction fan Sam Moskowitz, documenting the early history of science-fiction fandom. Moskowitz' hardcover book, published by the Atlanta Science-Fiction Organization Press in 1954, featured a powerful black and white design created by Frank R. Paul. Moskowitz's preservation copy signed to Paul in 1954 states "To Frank R. Paul—

Above: Frank R. Paul at work for Hugo Gernsback, at the offices of SCIENCE FICTION +, circa 1953. Photograph courtesy of the collection of Sam Moskowitz.

Opposite: *Frank R. Paul,* cover recreation commission used for AMAZING FORRIES, Metropolis Publications, Hollywood, California (printed by Warren Publications), November 1976.

Whose illustrations, more than any other man's, symbolize the true spirit of science fiction."

Unfortunately, bleak days lay ahead for the pulp-magazine market. By the mid 1950s, almost all science-fiction pulp titles had ceased publication or altered format to the new, smaller, digest-sized magazine. The paperback book had also become a popular format for many new science-fiction authors entering the field and new artists were employed to keep up with painting covers for them. Many of these younger artists brought with them a more modern or abstract approach to science-fiction art, which was encouraged and well-received by publishers and readers alike. Paul's work didn't seem to fit into that scene at all and he spent more time illustrating text books. In 1952, Paul moved back to Bergen County, where he rented an apartment located at 700 Cedar Lane, Teaneck, New Jersey. By this time, his wife, suffering from the illness of glaucoma for a few years, was almost totally blind. On March 1, 1953, Paul delivered a speech at the meeting of the Eastern Science-Fiction Association, the oldest science-fiction club in the New York and New Jersey area. The following year Paul did his only science-fiction fanzine cover up to this point in time—artwork for James V. Taurasi's *Fantasy Times* for the special No. 200 issue in June 1954.

In 1953, with Sam Moskowitz serving as Managing Editor, Hugo Gernsback returned to edit and publish the first "slick" science-fiction magazine the world had ever seen. The new monthly was titled *Science-Fiction Plus* and debuted at the newsstands in February 1953. The magazine had great enthusiasm and ideas behind it, and featured some of the top writers in the country. Frank R. Paul returned as Gernsback's Art Director and provided several beautiful cover and back cover paintings,

along with interior illustrations. Paul's artwork in these last few Gernsback magazines was extraordinary! The sixty-nine year old artist was inspired and obviously happy to once again be working with his old boss. He seemed to put an extra measure of technique and effort into all the illustrations featured. He employed the use of an airbrush to create better shading effects and to help soften the edge of a line, thus adding a greater sense of depth to both his color cover paintings and black and white interiors.

Paul had always been known for putting great detail into his drawings. However, the images

Above: Frank R. Paul at an early science-fiction meeting, circa 1950 with two unidentified fans. Photo courtesy of the collection of Sam Moskowitz.

Opposite: Family portrait of Frank R. Paul, circa 1950, photograph courtesy of Joan C. Engle. © Copyright the family of Frank R. Paul.

produced for *Science-Fiction Plus* were almost photographic and had a tonal quality, unlike much of his earlier work. Many of the interior illustrations were in point of fact black and white paintings! Unfortunately the magazine only lasted seven issues but for the next ten years the artist continued to provide drawings and illustrations for Greenback's other magazines *Radio-Electronics* and *Sexology*. He also turned out a number of illustrations for Greenback's annual Christmas card publication called *Forecast. Forecast* was a small (6" x 5") pocket sized 28 page (counting covers) pamphlet that was

published for Christmas of 1951 through 1965, each issue featuring cover and interior illustrations for the various featured articles by Paul (except the last three issues which featured artwork by Alex Schomburg after Paul's death). Before *Forecast,* Gernsback's Christmas pamphlets were one-shot titles such as his 1949 *Quip* which was a "Special Mars Number," featuring a charming Martian-Alien cover with over a dozen interior illustrations.

It seems evident at this time that Paul only continued to do science-fiction illustration because he loved doing it, not because he needed money. As noted by Sam Moskowitz, in the fifth issue of *Science-Fiction Plus:* "Although Paul is a famed name in the science-fiction world, he is as well known as an architectural and mechanical draftsman, having designed the exterior of the famous Johnson & Johnson plant at Brunswick, New Jersey." One would think Paul made lots of money doing architectural work for building projects he was involved in, yet his family confirms that he "never really made any serious money" illustrating during his lifetime. With the death of *Science-Fiction Plus,* Paul basically left the field of science-fiction and became more heavily involved with other projects. He never retired, and in 1957, he was asked to paint the cover of *Satellite Science Fiction* for the December issue. Paul decided to paint an image of what he called the ultimate earth satellite space station of the future. It was most appropriate that he selected this theme, due to the fact that twenty-eight years earlier he had painted the very first image of an "Earth satellite" on the cover of the August 1929 issue of *Science Wonder Stories.*

In 1959, after suffering from a gall bladder surgery where he was kept in the hospital for a week or so, the doctors advised Paul to stay immobilized for two weeks. After this episode, he rode a bus into New York City where he delivered illustrations to various accounts. Paul did lose one or two important clients during his stay at the hospital and he began a project entitled "Hot War-Cold War," a series of small paintings which he hoped to sell after getting back on his feet after his surgery. He was determined to deliver his work on time, and never missed a deadline!

It seems unconceivable, as popular as Frank R. Paul was with science-fiction fandom, that no one had ever offered to commission science-fiction works directly from him for their private collection. It is well documented that the great Edgar Rice Burroughs book illustrator, J. Allen St. John, enjoyed private art commissions toward the end of his career. In 1959, Paul was contacted by one of the greatest, most enthusiastic science-fiction fans of the previous four decades for Frank R. Paul's work—Forrest J Ackerman. Ackerman proposed to pay for two commissioned paintings. Each painting would contain an element of personal content and great importance to collector Ackerman, dating back to his early teens. The first painting, and the once most dear to his heart, was the very first issue of *Amazing Stories,* that he had picked up off the newsstands in October 1926. Ackerman has always said that the magazine spoke to him "take me home, Little Boy, and you will love me." Always the punster, Ackerman had Paul change the cover title from *Amazing Stories* to *Amazing Forries,* with the cover date of October 2026, and at the bottom of the painting added "This is Your Life Forrest J Ackerman." This first commissioned work, almost identical to the October 1926 *Amazing* cover, has the lettering of "4 S J +" added to the side of the space ship. In between the two lobster-like aliens, Forry himself appears, instead of the original figure on the cover.

The second commission used "gold-leaf background paint, with Paul recreating the cover for the August 1924 issue of *Science and Invention.* This special issue had featured an incredible cover by famed pulp artist Howard V. Brown, depicting a Martian excavating and blasting rock formations. Inside this issue is found two informative articles about Martians and the planet Mars itself. These articles, titled "Evolution on Mars" and "Mars as Closest Point to Earth," both feature stunning ink wash illustrations by Frank R. Paul. Ackerman, who celebrated his 90th birthday in 2006, was one of the country's most enthusiastic fans and historians of science fiction, persuaded Paul to repaint this cover with the new title of *Martian Science Fiction,* depicting Ackerman himself in a futuristic spacesuit, next to the Martian, both standing in the middle of a crystal-like plant life form. In a handwritten letter to Ackerman, dated November 22nd, 1960, Paul stated in part "Sorry to keep you waiting so long, but you know I have a lot of contractual work with stiff deadlines attached to each job, and of course Gernsback's yearly spasm of Christmas Card had to come in between. However I put a little extra work on the picture of my favorite fan as you will find. I showed you as a real Space Captain in full uniform. I'll send you the Gold one as soon as I get it done, in the meantime let me congratulate you on your classy personal card, out of this world."

In 1976, the first painting appeared on the cover of a special one-shot publication about Forrest J Ackerman (written by Forry) titled *Amazing Forries,* published by Warren Publications. This first painting is now on permanent display in Paul Allen's Science-Fiction Hall of Fame Museum in Seattle, Washington. The second painting of Ackerman and the Martian is now in a private collection.

The only other private commission that Paul encountered came from none other than Sam Moskowitz, who in 1960 talked the artist into doing a special painting for his wife Christine. Sam wanted to surprise his wife (who collected elephant figures and works of art) with a special painting by Frank R. Paul based on his previous back cover "Life on Other Worlds" series for *Amazing Stories* and *Fantastic Adventures.* Paul did a terrific painting where the crew of a space ship (having made its landing on an alien lake) are embarking onto land transferred by giant elephants. This painting was shortly thereafter used as the back cover for the 35th Anniversary issue of *Amazing Stories* for April of 1961. Paul also did the handsome front cover illustration. The inside back cover noted "This may be the first time in science fiction that one artist is represented by a full-color

Frank R. Paul, undated design for Hugo Gernsback commission for design on a building project entitled "20th Century Globe," circa 1950. Photograph courtesy of the Sam Moskowitz collection.

illustration on both the front and back covers of the same issue of a magazine. If so, it is logical that the honor should fall to Frank R. Paul, considered by many to be the dean of science-fiction artists." When this magazine was published by Ziff-Davis, the artist was seventy-seven years old.

Hugo Gernsback and Frank R. Paul were both invited as guests of honor at the Newark meeting of the Eastern Science-Fiction League Association in 1961. By 1961, Paul had been active in the field as a professional artist for over 45 years, and to many science-fiction fans he was over the hill, or completely out of touch with what many considered the *modern* impulses of artists such as Richard Powers, John Schoenherr, or Paul Lehr. However, to

Sam Moskowitz, who was the premier science-fiction historian of his time (and who also had his years of experience with both Gernsback and Paul culminating during 1953 with the short run for *Science-Fiction Plus*), and still part-time acting president of the ESFA League, this was an excellent opportunity for the public and science-fiction fans to spend an afternoon with two of their greatest figures. Joe Wrzos, who attended this meeting, confirms that on March 12, 1961, the records for ESFA confirm that Hugo Gernsback, Frank R. Paul, Norman Lobsenz (editorial director at that time for *Amazing Stories),* and Cele Goldsmith (an editorial assistant) were all in attendance for a special "Salute to *Amazing Stories*" ESFA meeting. Mr. Wrzos was an editor for *Amazing Stories* for a short period of time himself, and also a close friend to Sam Moskowitz, as well as being a life-long Paul fan, and he was thrilled to be attending this special meeting. Wrzos remembers on that afternoon after Frank R. Paul spoke that he as the *younger fan* went up to the *older veteran* and asked the following question: "Mr. Paul, I've noticed that many of your human figures during the 1920s illustrations have a strong resemblance to Japanese watercolor wood-cuts from the Ukiyo-e period, specifically to artists such as Hiroshige and Hokusai, am I right?" The old veteran looked the younger fan in the eye, and with a twinkle in his own eye said "Oh yes, but I was influenced by all of that kind of thing back then!"

This chance encounter between Frank R. Paul with a seasoned science-fiction fan/pro and their short conversation reveals much about the artist. For while Paul was often criticized for having stiff figures in his illustrations, or designing paintings where too much action was taking place in too small of a space the truth was far from the easy clichés bantered about by many science-fiction fans. Frank R. Paul was a gifted artist, coming to America from Europe and preserving his own traditions while intellectually taking in the surrounding new culture of the American landscape. Paul was perfectly positioned in his lifetime to engage in the development of a new visual language, and as he grew into this new culture, his own visual

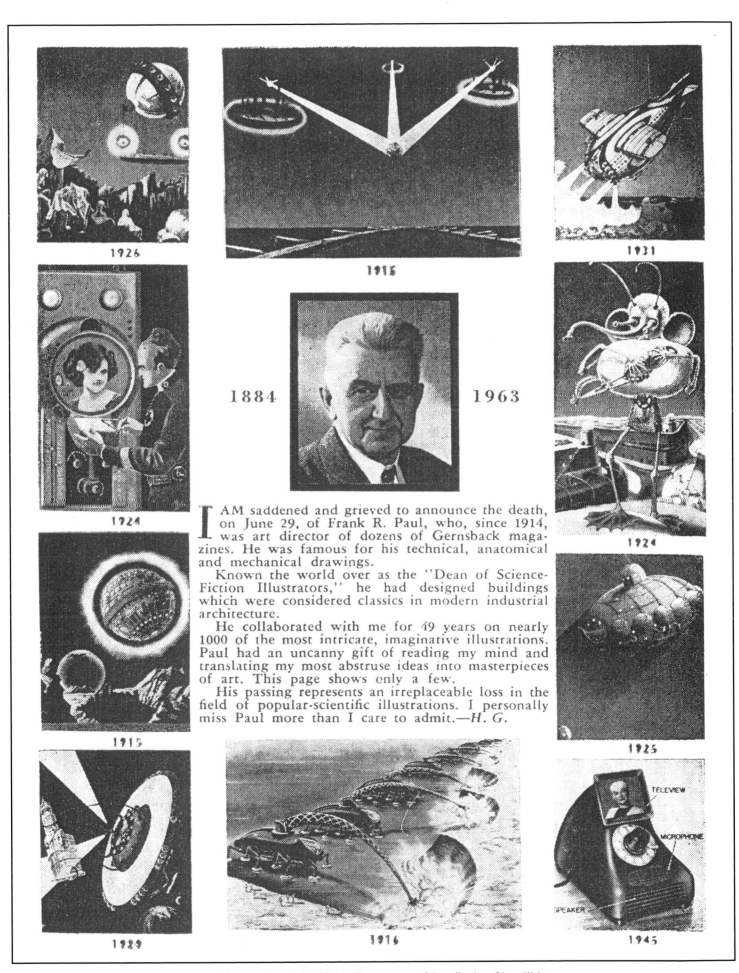

1926

1915

1931

1924

1884   1963

1924

I AM saddened and grieved to announce the death, on June 29, of Frank R. Paul, who, since 1914, was art director of dozens of Gernsback magazines. He was famous for his technical, anatomical and mechanical drawings.

Known the world over as the ''Dean of Science-Fiction Illustrators,'' he had designed buildings which were considered classics in modern industrial architecture.

He collaborated with me for 49 years on nearly 1000 of the most intricate, imaginative illustrations. Paul had an uncanny gift of reading my mind and translating my most abstruse ideas into masterpieces of art. This page shows only a few.

His passing represents an irreplaceable loss in the field of popular-scientific illustrations. I personally miss Paul more than I care to admit.—*H. G.*

1915

1925

1929

1916

1945

Frank R. Paul Back Cover tribute from FORECAST 1964, Hugo Gernsback Publisher. Photo courtesy of the collection of Jerry Weist.

language extended itself as the very foundations of science fiction were being formed, and then broken and changed again and again by each succeeding generation. Artists as diverse as Jack Kirby have paid their tributes and acknowledged the influence of Paul's early work on their formative years. Alex Schomburg, Elliott Dold, Leo Moray, Julian Krupa, Robert Fuqua, Hans Wesso, and even the great Virgil Finlay all took something from Paul's linear lessons, and brought that dynamic sense of wonder into their own science-fiction and fantasy illustrations. There is a time and place for everything, and every person, and Frank R. Paul was perfectly placed into the fabric of the very beginnings of science-fiction's culture as it expanded outward to embrace every part of the world. He now stands secure as our visual grandfather, a man who brought the future into our lives. And his vision of the future remains with us to this day.

In an article on Paul, written by Forrest J Ackerman, along with personal comments from various long-time professionals in the science-fiction field, Gerry de la Ree, the respected author and collector of science-fiction and fantasy original art, had this to say about visiting the elderly artist during the last few years of his life: "In 1957, during my years as a sportswriter/editor for the *Bergen Evening Record* of Hackensack, New Jersey, I discovered that Paul was living only a few miles from my office in Teaneck. I spent an afternoon with him and started a friendship that ended only with his death in 1963. I did an interview with him at that time, but the lasting impression I have is not of his many fascinating drawings and covers but of a gentle, smiling white-haired man who seemed to ooze friendship from every pore. His Spartan apartment had no great Paul art hanging on the walls or piles of artwork on the floor; but for his drawing board and paints, there was no indication of the great impact he had on the science-fiction field three decades earlier. He seemed embarrassed that I looked upon him as someone extraordinary. But extraordinary he was, with a capital X, as his work attests."

On June 29, 1963, at the age of 79, Frank R. Paul passed away. He had just completed an illustration for Gernsback Publications that evening. It was the end of an era in science-fiction illustration. There can be little doubt that his influence has been felt by many over the years, especially the artists who followed later. Paul was the first artist to blaze a path through the uncharted waters of early science-fiction magazine illustration, producing beautiful, bold images laced with a great sense of wonder, so identified with the early years of the field. It's symbolic that this artist who was joined spiritually at the hip to his mentor and publisher Hugo Gernsback in the world of science fiction spent his last evening creating an illustration for his old friend.

In the 1964 issue of his *Forecast* Christmas card magazine, Hugo Gernsback wrote an obituary on Frank R. Paul, an excerpt of which reads:

"He collaborated with me for 49 years on nearly 1,000 of the most intricate, imaginative illustrations. Paul had an uncanny gift of reading my mind and translating my most abstruse ideas into masterpieces of art. His passing represents an irreplaceable loss in the field of popular-scientific illustrations. I personally miss Paul more than I care to admit."

It is fitting to end this short history with a quote from Frank R. Paul's speech delivered at a March 1, 1953, meeting of the Eastern Science-Fiction Association:

"A friend asked me once, on seeing a picture I drew of the inhabitants of a strange world, 'How do you know that people on that world look like that?' Well, the answer was: 'Simple, I was there.' Of course that brought a laugh, but for all intents and purposes it was quite a truthful and logical answer. You see, with a little imagination you can transfer yourself to any place in the universe traveling on thought waves, the speed of which makes the speed of light look like parking. I am sure you find just as much fun and fascination in exploring strange worlds as I do. To my mind, the best science-fiction stories do not necessarily deal with horrors, murders and destruction, but rather those which stimulate our imagination in exploring the wonders of the future in every branch of science. And what the future holds in store for us is both exciting and fun."

Opposite: Frank R. Paul, original painting for the cover to THE THIRTEENTH WORLD SCIENCE FICTION CONVENTION PROGRAM BOOKLET, the "Clevention" for Labor Day Weekend of 1955. (This was the first full color cover for a World Convention Booklet). Attendance for this convention was 380 fans, slightly less than the Paul painting would suggest. Painting from the collection of Robert Weinberg.

August

BROADCAST WRNY STATION

AMAZING STORIES

25 Cents

HUGO GERNSBACK
EDITOR

Stories by
H. G. Wells
Edward Elmer Smith
Philip Francis Nowlan

EXPERIMENTER PUBLISHING COMPANY. 230 FIFTH AVENUE, NEW YORK

Frank R. Paul, AMAZING STORIES cover illustration, 1928. Some believe this cover to be the first depiction of Buck Rogers.

FATHER OF THE SCIENCE-FICTION ILLUSTRATORS

by

GERRY DE LA REE

Eighty-two years ago two men pooled their talents to give the world its first all-science-fiction magazine, setting the stage for a new publishing field that is today a flourishing one. Those men were Hugo Gernsback, editor and publisher, and Frank R. Paul, an Austrian-born artist who was destined to become known as the Father of the Science-Fiction Illustrators. And while his artistic ventures were many and varied in a long and busy career, Paul gained his greatest and most lasting fame in the filed of imaginative fiction.

Paul did considerable work for Gernsback's magazines, *Electric Experimenter*, *Modern Electrics*, and *Science and Invention*. It was in the pages of these publications, and to a lesser extent in Gernsback's *Radio News*, that modern science fiction got its start for Gernsback, a born dreamer, inserted occasional fictional works in the pages of his fact magazines. For example, the August 1923 issue of *Science and Invention* was labeled "Scientific Issue" and carried a half dozen science fiction-type stories.

Finally, in 1926, Gernsback took the plunge and brought out the world's first all-science-fiction magazine, *Amazing Stories*. The cover, illustrating Jules Verne's "Off On A Comet," and all the interior drawings as well as the magazine's distinctive logo were from the pen and brush of Frank R. Paul.

Amazing Stories flourished for the next three years under Gernsback's editorship and with Paul handling all of the artwork. At first the stories were mainly reprints of the old masters such as Jules Verne, H.G. Wells, and Edgar Allen Poe; gradually, however, new authors were developed. In 1929 Gernsback, like many other businessmen of the day, found himself in receivership as a result of the stock market crash. He lost his magazine chain and radio station and another publisher took over *Amazing Stories*.

Frank R. Paul, cover illustration for EVERYDAY MECHANICS for July 1930, Gernsback Publications. Photo courtesy of the collection of Jerry Weist.

Gerry de la Ree was a science fiction art publisher, dealer, collector, and, by occupation, newspaper sports journalist. This article was edited and condensed from *The Bergen Evening Record*.

Frank R. Paul, original painting for the cover to WONDER STORIES, June 1935, gouache on board, signed lower left. One of the most striking of Paul's early paintings, from Laurence Manning's "Seeds From Space." From the Korshak collection.

deeply impressed by what I still think is one of the greatest pictures of its type to have been done by any illustrator, although it was not precisely science fiction. That was Paul's picture of Manhattan with the lid off. It was a perfect example of an artist who takes his research seriously."

Paul never had any regrets for the years he spent in science fiction. "I always enjoyed reading and illustrating the stories."

His science interest in the future was evident in a speech he delivered at the first World Science Fiction Convention held in New York in 1939 where Paul, as Guest of Honor, said in part:

"Two thousand years ago a meeting such as this, with all these rebellious, adventurous minds would have been looked upon as a very serious psychological phenomenon, and the leaders would have been put in chains or at least burned at the stake. But today it may well be considered the healthiest sign of youthful, wide-awake minds—to discuss subjects beyond the range of the average provincial mind.

"The science-fiction fan may well be called the advance-guard of progress. . . . He is intensely interested in everything going on around him, differing radically from his critic. His critic is hemmed in by a small provincial horizon of accepted orthodoxy and humdrum realities and either does not care or is too lazy to reach beyond that horizon.

"Once in a while we also find eminent scientists throwing cold water on our enthusiasms. For instance, the other day Dr. Robert Millikan said we should stop dreaming about atomic power and solar power. We feel, as much as we love the doctor as one of the foremost scientists of the day, because he cannot see its realization or gets tired of research is no reason to give up hope that some scientists of the future might not attack the problem and ride it. What seems utterly impossible today may be commonplace tomorrow."

How prophetic.

During his career, Paul did many things in the illustrating vein. He once served as cartoonist for the *Jersey Journal*, he had a large spread in the first issue of *Life* magazine back in 1936, did architectural

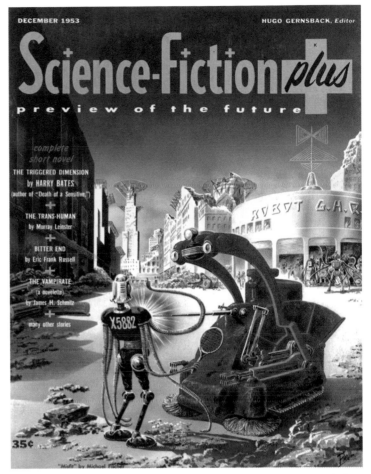

Above: *Frank R. Paul*, cover design for SCIENCE FICTION PLUS, December of 1953, the final cover done for a Gernsback publication, by this time Paul was using airbrush techniques and his painted work had taken on a less linear and more painterly style.

work, and during World War II did designing for the government.

His work of illustrating text books for colleges and high schools is something he did off and on during most of his career. Each book called for several hundred separate illustrations, and the topics included biology, physics, chemistry, and history. It was a laborious and taxing job, but a rather routine one for a man who pioneered in a sphere where imagination and inventiveness are necessities.

Paul could not help but be proud in the realization that many of today's science-fiction artists and authors were weaned on his illustrations. An admired and respected forerunner, Paul is indeed the dean of the science-fiction illustrators and, as such, has left his impression etched indelibly on an ever expanding field that admittedly owes him its eternal gratitude.

Frank R. Paul, original painting for the back cover to AMAZING STORIES, Giant 35th Anniversary Issue, April 1961, gouache on board, signed lower left, from the Collection of Sam Moskowitz. This painting constitutes the only other known private commission to Paul (the other two being bought by Forrest J Ackerman). In this commission, Sam had Paul paint a scene from his popular "Life on Other Worlds" theme that had graced previous AMAZING back covers in the 1940s, using elephants (Sam's wife Christine had a collection of elephant statues and illustrations) and, since Moskowitz had a close friendship and professional working relationship with the AMAZING editor and publisher, he allowed this painting to be used for the back cover.

FRANK R. PAUL REMEMBERED

by

SAM MOSKOWITZ

There are many students of science fiction that doubt that *Amazing Stories* would have ever established itself at all if it had not been its good fortune to possess the services of the illustrator Frank R. Paul in the formative days. As the first of the science-fiction magazines, *Amazing Stories* had to effectively project its persona to the public, and the only way that could be done was through cover and interior art and Paul's genius. Paul rested on the fact that his work accurately reflected the spirit of science fiction and thus the public instantly grasped the content of *Amazing Stories* from his renditions. Beyond that, his work possessed a provocativeness, and a sense of wonder, that enticed readership.

Paul met Hugo Gernsback in 1914 and immediately began illustrating for Gernsback's *Electrical Experimenter*, Gernsback published many science-fiction "mysteries" in that magazine and Paul's extensive training in architectural and mechanical draftsmanship gave his illustrations an authenticity that few other illustrators possessed.

When *Amazing Stories* was undertaken in 1926, Paul's talents as an expert calligrapher were also brought into play to design the famous comet-tale logo. When he had completed the lettering, he sketched in his idea of a cover illustration for Jules Verne's "Off on a Comet" and Gernsback decided to give him a chance at full-color work. The results were a series of imaginative renderings that have since become classics in this field and helped to elevate *Amazing Stories* to an almost immediate success. Paul's strongest points were his visualization of imaginary machinery which looked like they would actually work, his remarkable astronomical paintings which were the prototypes of the ones made famous by Chesley Bonestal, his talent for outré, other-worldly creatures and the cartoonists knack of giving them expression and personality. Paul drew thousands of space ships, but he never drew the

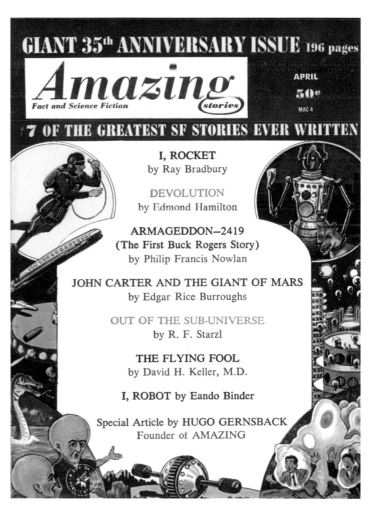

Frank R. Paul, cover design for painting to AMAZING STORIES, Giant 35th Anniversary Issue, April 1961, Ziff Davis Publications.

Sam Moskowitz was considered the foremost authority and scholar of his day on science fiction. He was inducted into the New Jersey literary hall of fame in 1987.

Frank R. Paul, original painting for the cover to WONDER STORIES, August 1931, gouache on illustration board, signed on the lower left, illustrating "The 35th Millennium," by Arthur F. Stangland. From the Korshak collection.

FRANK R. PAUL SELECTED SCIENCE-FICTION COVER GALLERY

JULY
1929

AUGUST
1929

SEPTEMBER
1929

OCTOBER
1929

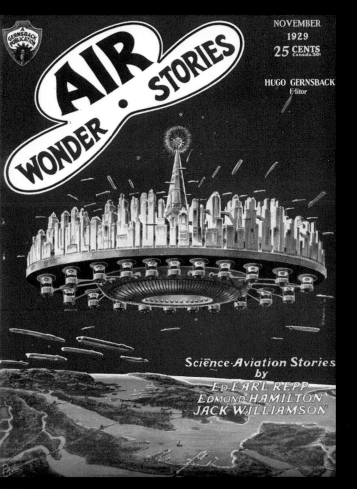

NOVEMBER
1929

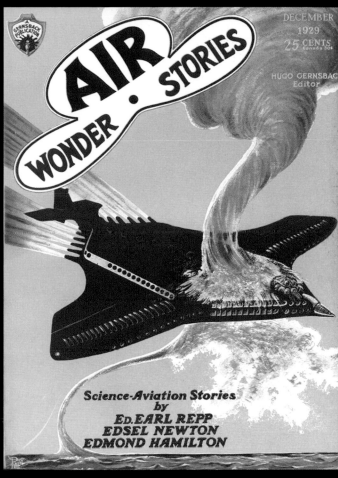

DECEMBER
1929

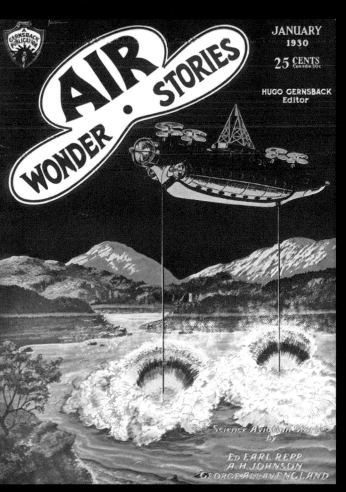

JANUARY

FEBRUARY

MARCH
1930

APRIL
1930

MAY
1930

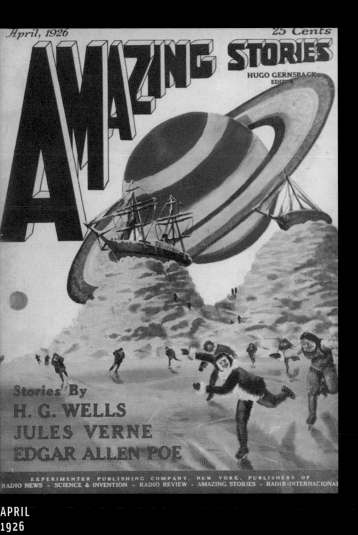

APRIL
1926

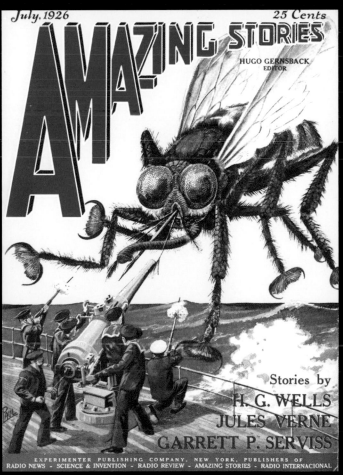

MAY
1926

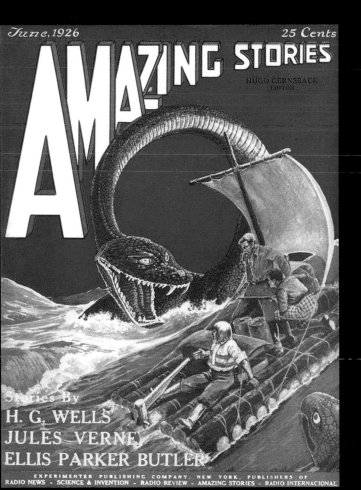

JUNE

JULY

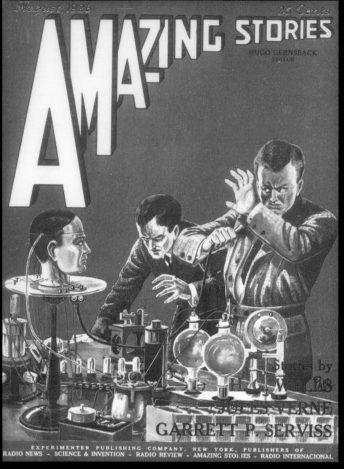

AUGUST
1926

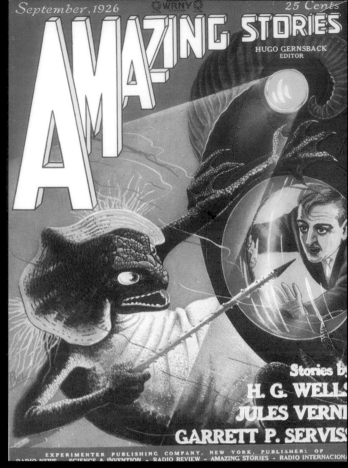

SEPTEMBER
1926

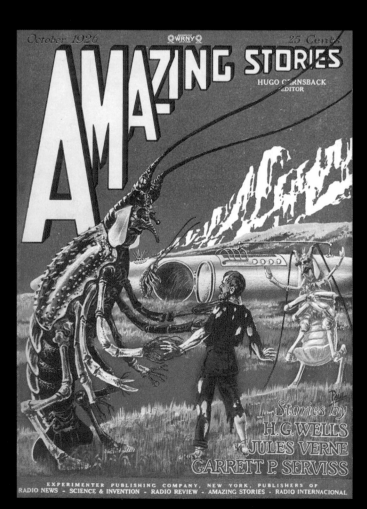

OCTOBER
1926

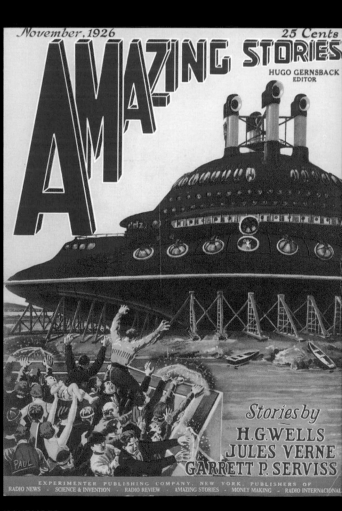

NOVEMBER
1926

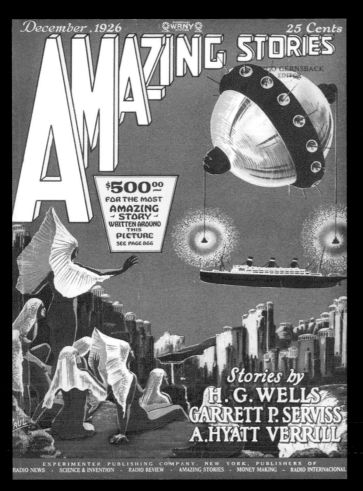

DECEMBER
1926

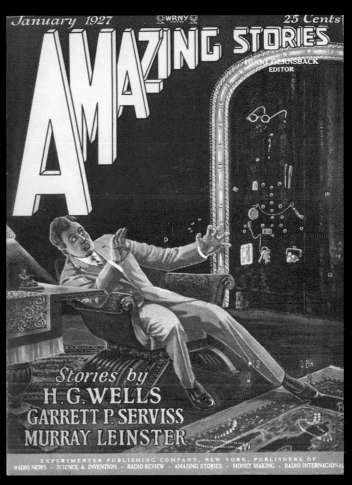

JANUARY
1927

FEBRUARY
1927

MARCH
1927

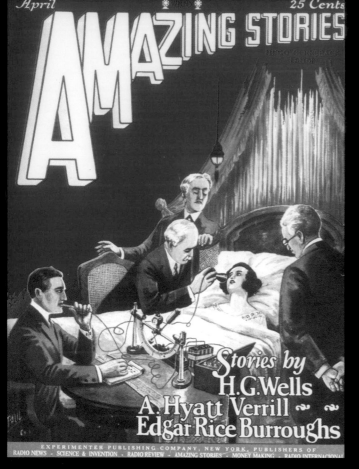

**APRIL
1927**

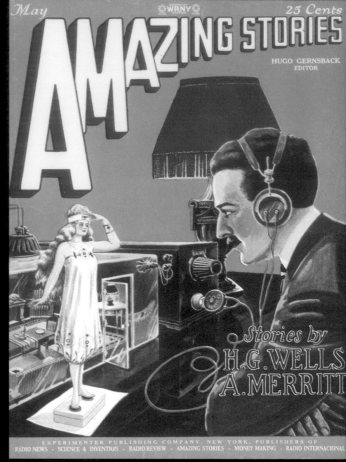

**MAY
1927**

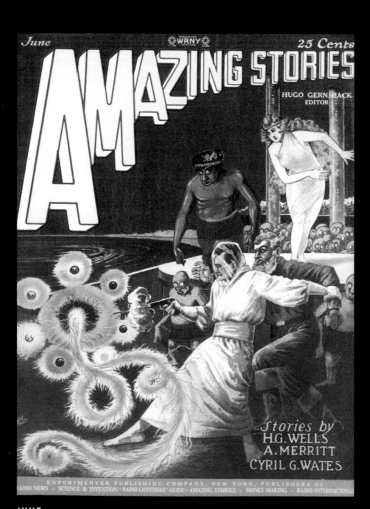

**JUNE
1927**

**JULY
1927**

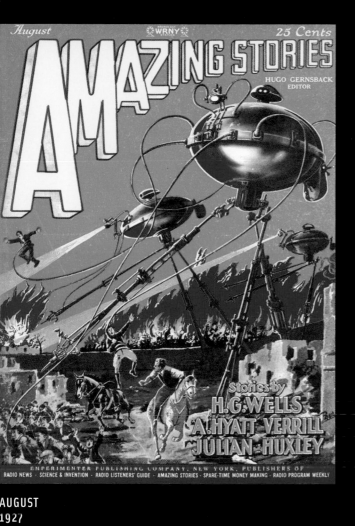

AUGUST
1927

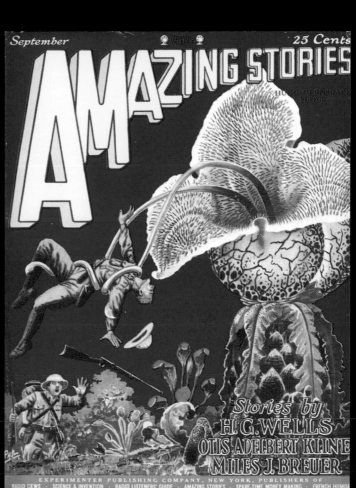

SEPTEMBER
1927

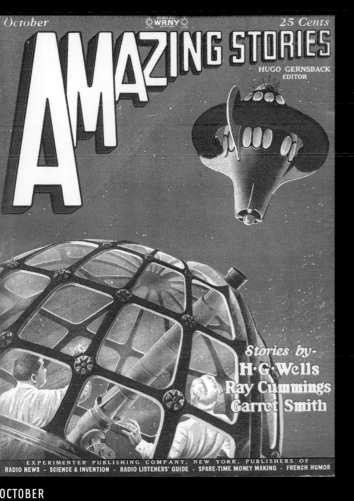

OCTOBER
1927

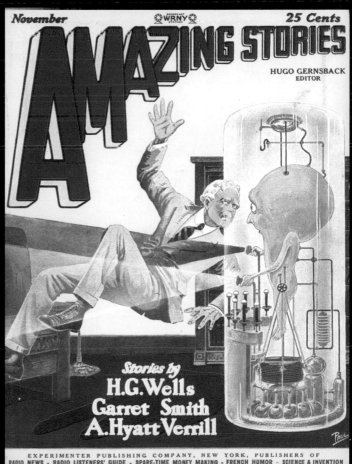

NOVEMBER
1927

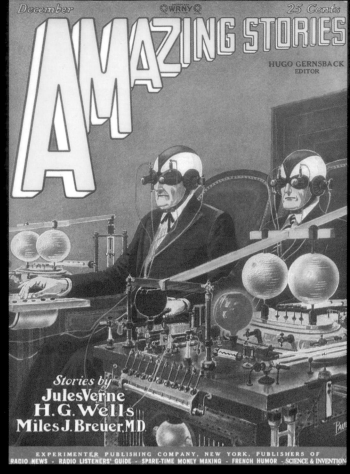

DECEMBER
1927

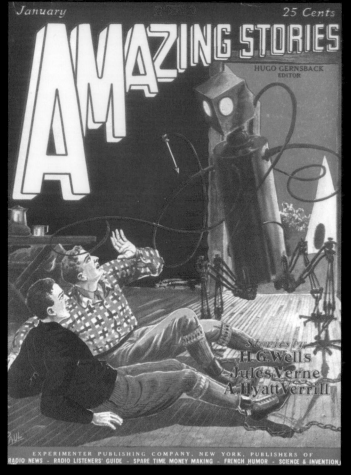

JANUARY
1928

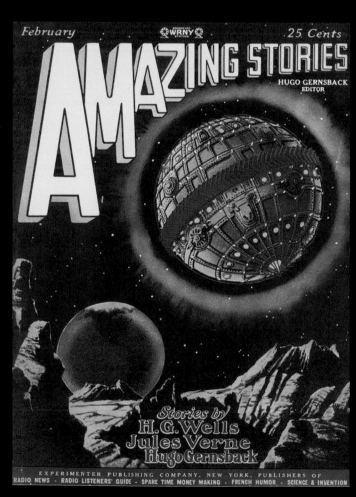

FEBRUARY
1928

MARCH
1928

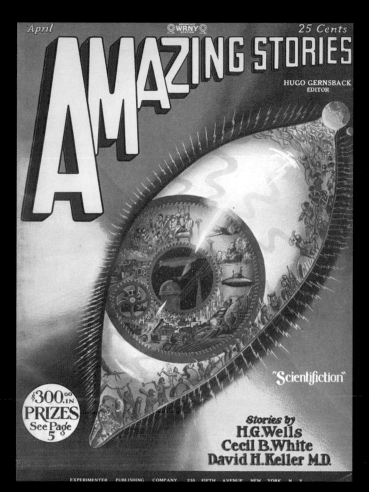

APRIL
1928

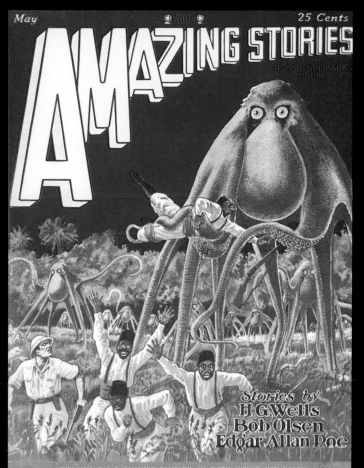

MAY
1928

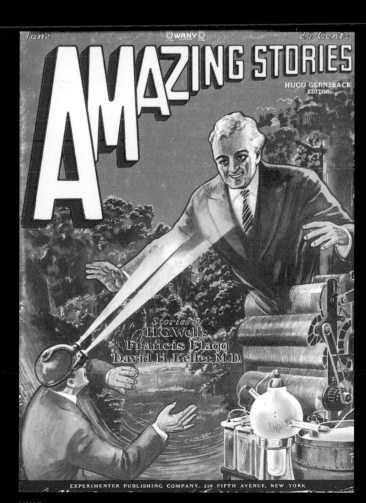

JUNE
1928

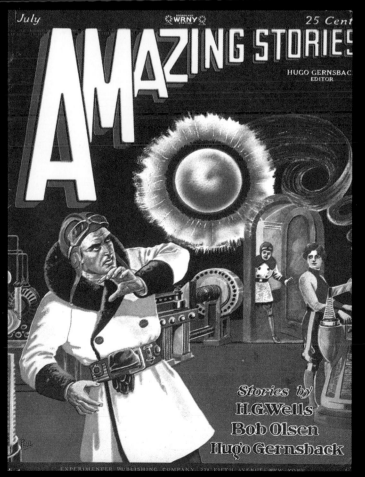

JULY
1928

COVER GALLERY

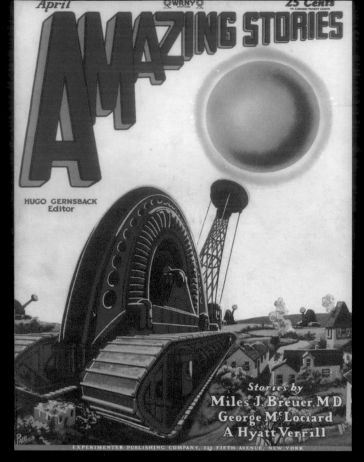

APRIL
1929

MAY
1929

JUNE
1929

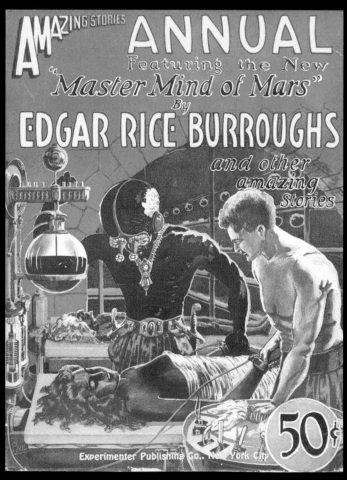

ANNUAL NO. 1
1928

APRIL
1961

APRIL (BACK COVER)
1961

SPRING
1928

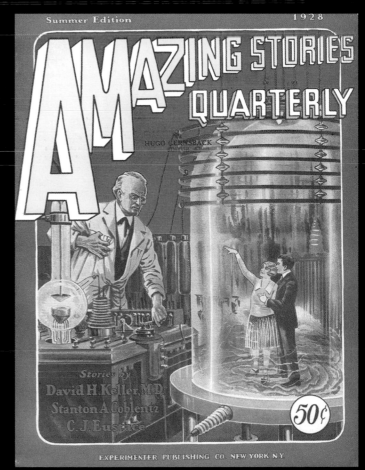

SUMMER
1928

Interplanetary Number

"THE MARK OF THE METEOR"
By Ray Cummings

WINTER
1931

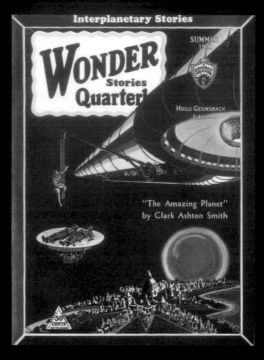

SUMMER
1931

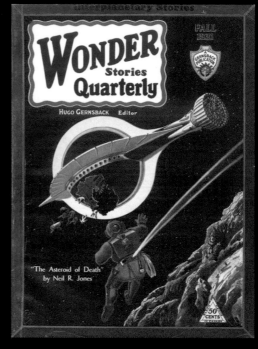

FALL
1931

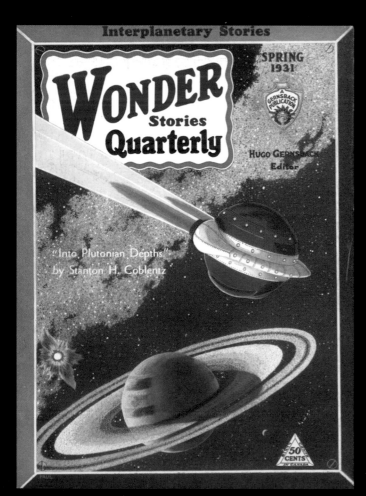

Interplanetary Stories

"Into Plutonian Depths"
by Stanton H. Coblentz

SPRING
1931

WINTER
1932

GIANT 35th ANNIVERSARY ISSUE 196 pages

Amazing
Fact and Science Fiction *stories*

APRIL
50¢
MAC 4

7 OF THE GREATEST SF STORIES EVER WRITTEN

I, ROCKET
by Ray Bradbury

DEVOLUTION
by Edmond Hamilton

ARMAGEDDON–2419
(The First Buck Rogers Story)
by Philip Francis Nowlan

JOHN CARTER AND THE GIANT OF MARS
by Edgar Rice Burroughs

OUT OF THE SUB-UNIVERSE
by R. F. Starzl

THE FLYING FOOL
by David H. Keller, M.D.

I, ROBOT by Eando Binder

Special Article by HUGO GERNSBACK
Founder of AMAZING

APRIL
1961

APRIL (BACK COVER)
1961

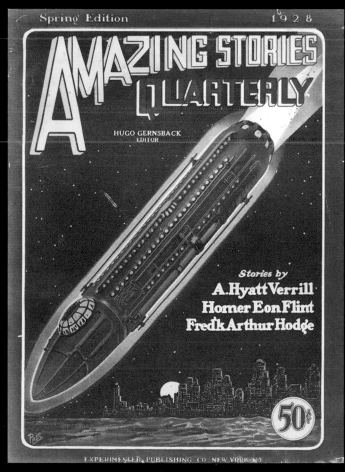

SPRING
1928

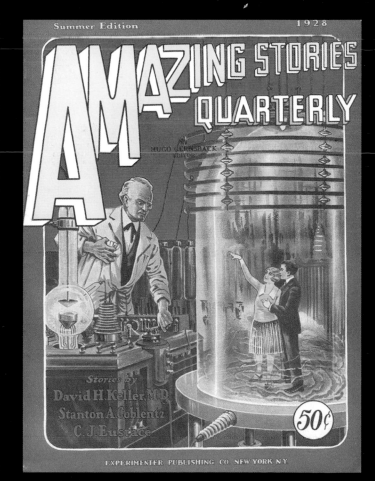

SUMMER
1928

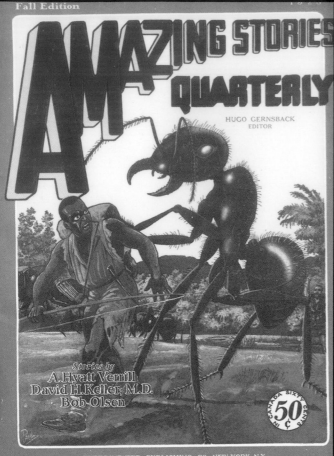

FALL
1928

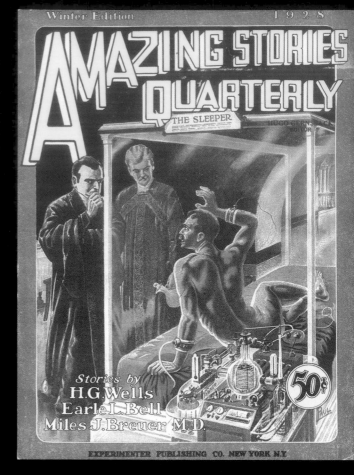

WINTER
1928

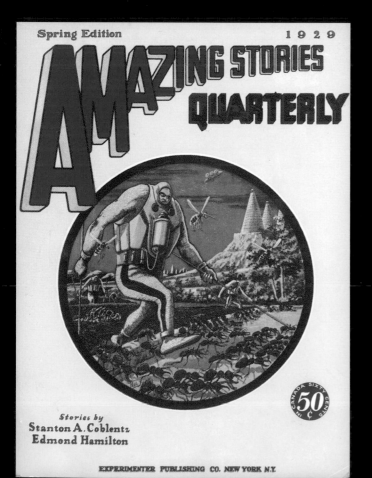

SPRING
1929

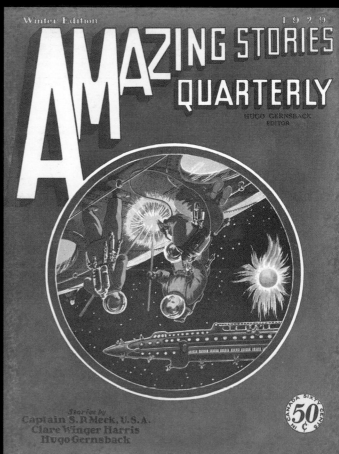

WINTER
1929

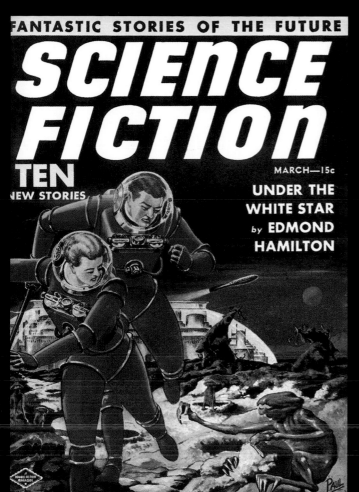

FANTASTIC STORIES OF THE FUTURE

SCIENCE FICTION

TEN
NEW STORIES

MARCH—15c

UNDER THE WHITE STAR
by EDMOND HAMILTON

MARCH
1939

SCIENCE FICTION

15¢
JUNE

WHERE ETERNITY ENDS
a complete novel
by EANDO BINDER
also
MANLY WADE WELLMAN
THOMAS S. GARDNER
and others

JUNE
1939

SCIENCE FICTION

THE GOD THAT SCIENCE MADE
by
LLOYD ARTHUR ESHBACH

also
ED EARL REPP
RAYMOND Z. GALLUN
EDMOND HAMILTON

15c
AUG.

AN INVADING SUN
the story behind the cover
by
EANDO BINDER

AUGUST
1939

SCIENCE FICTION

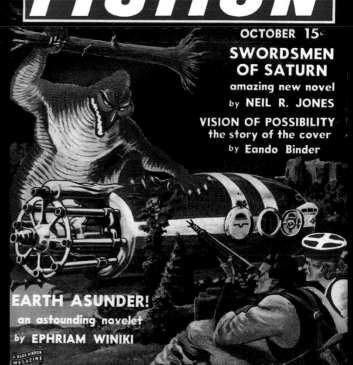

OCTOBER 15c

SWORDSMEN OF SATURN
amazing new novel
by NEIL R. JONES

VISION OF POSSIBILITY
the story of the cover
by Eando Binder

EARTH ASUNDER!
an astounding novelet
by EPHRIAM WINIKI

OCTOBER
1939

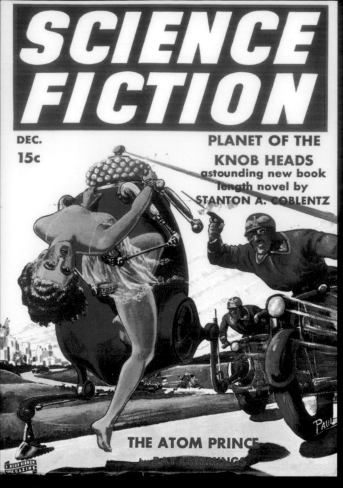

SCIENCE FICTION

DEC.
15c

PLANET OF THE
KNOB HEADS
astounding new book
length novel by
STANTON A. COBLENTZ

THE ATOM PRINCE

DECEMBER
1939

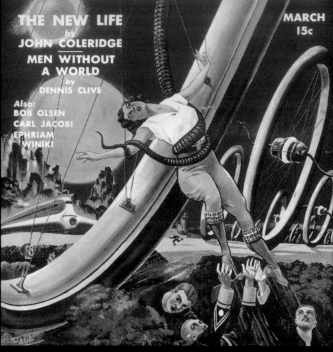

SCIENCE FICTION

MARCH
15c

THE NEW LIFE
by
JOHN COLERIDGE
MEN WITHOUT
A WORLD
by
DENNIS CLIVE

Also:
BOB OLSEN
CARL JACOBI
EPHRIAM
WINIKI

MARCH
1940

SCIENCE FICTION

THE VOICE COMMANDS
by DENNIS CLIVE

Also: NELSON S. BOND
PAUL EDMONDS
JOHN COLERIDGE

JUNE
15c

JUNE
1940

SCIENCE FICTION

THE MAN WHO
SOLD THE EARTH
by THORNTON AYRE

DEATH AND THE
DICTATOR
by RAYMOND Z. GALLUN
Also—
BOB OLSEN

OCTOBER   15c

OCTOBER
1940

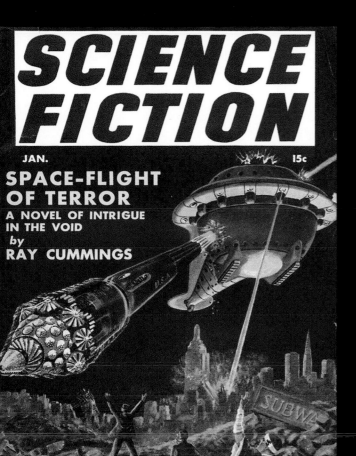

JANUARY
1941

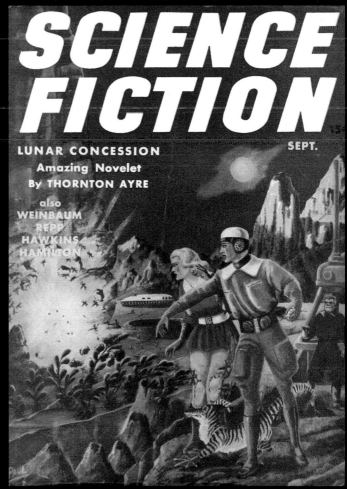

MARCH
1941

JUNE
1941

SEPTEMBER
1941

MAY
1953

AUGUST
1953

OCTOBER
1953

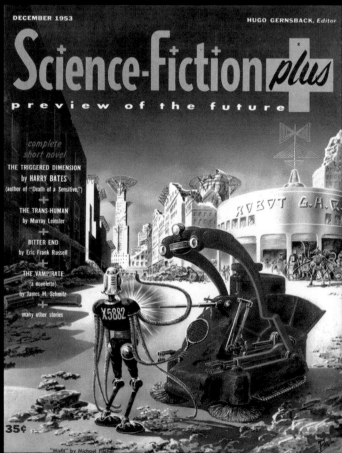

DECEMBER
1953

FALL
1929

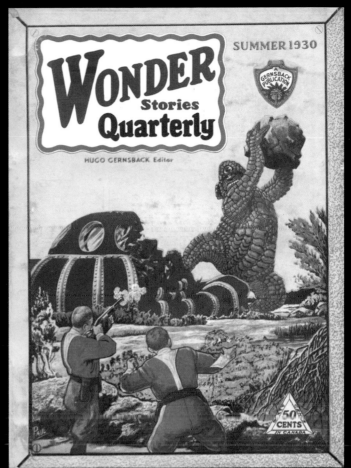

SUMMER
1930

WINTER
1930

SPRING
1930

FALL
1930

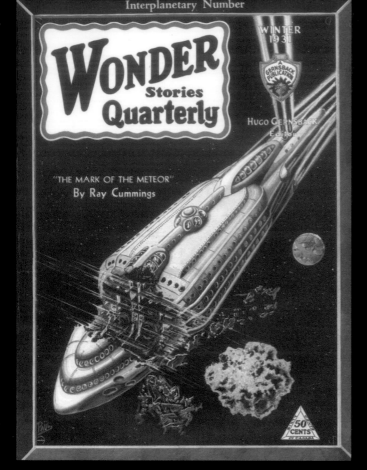

Interplanetary Number

WONDER Stories Quarterly

WINTER 1931

Hugo Gernsback Editor

"THE MARK OF THE METEOR"
By Ray Cummings

50 CENTS IN CANADA

WINTER
1931

Interplanetary Stories

WONDER Stories Quarterly

SUMMER 1931

Hugo Gernsback Editor

"The Amazing Planet"
by Clark Ashton Smith

SUMMER
1931

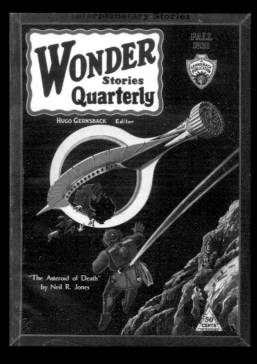

Interplanetary Stories

WONDER Stories Quarterly

FALL 1931

Gernsback Publication

Hugo Gernsback Editor

"The Asteroid of Death"
by Neil R. Jones

50 CENTS

FALL
1931

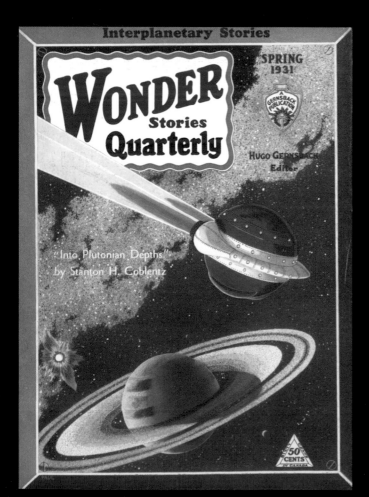

Interplanetary Stories

WONDER Stories Quarterly

SPRING 1931

Gernsback Publication

Hugo Gernsback Editor

"Into Plutonian Depths"
by Stanton H. Coblentz

50 CENTS IN CANADA

SPRING
1931

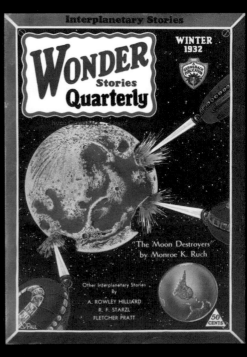

Interplanetary Stories

WONDER Stories Quarterly

WINTER 1932

Gernsback Publication

"The Moon Destroyers"
by Monroe K. Ruch

Other Interplanetary Stories
By
A. ROWLEY HILLIARD
R. F. STARZL
FLETCHER PRATT

50 CENTS

WINTER
1932

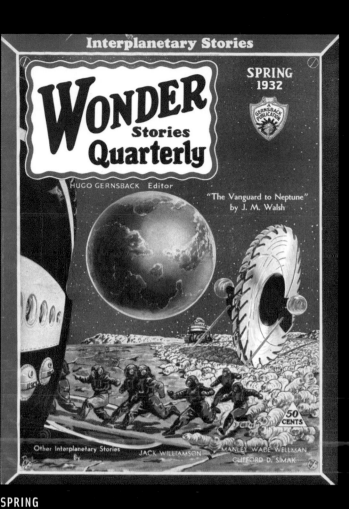

SPRING
1932

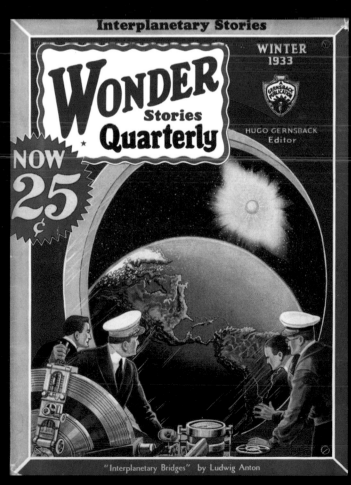

SUMMER
1932

FALL
1932

WINTER
1933

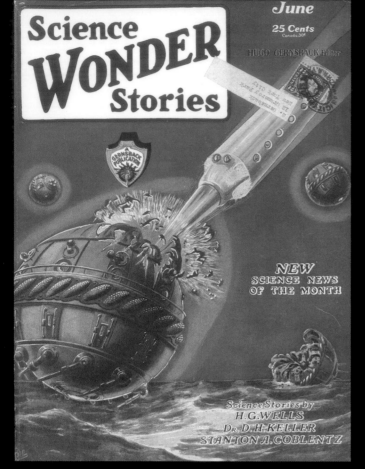

JUNE
1929

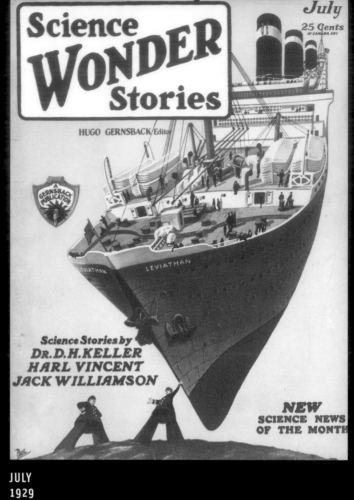

JULY
1929

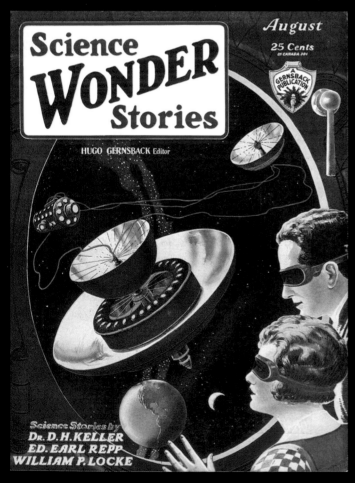

AUGUST
1929

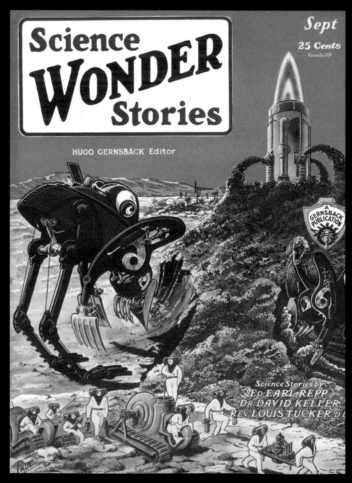

SEPTEMBER
1929

OCTOBER
1929

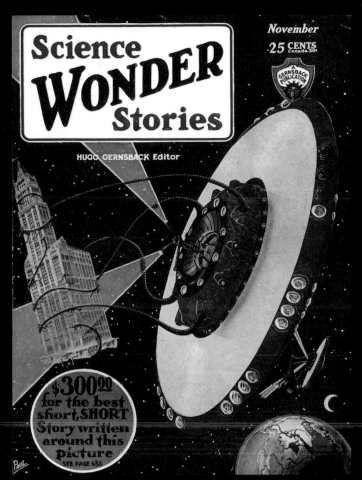

NOVEMBER
1929

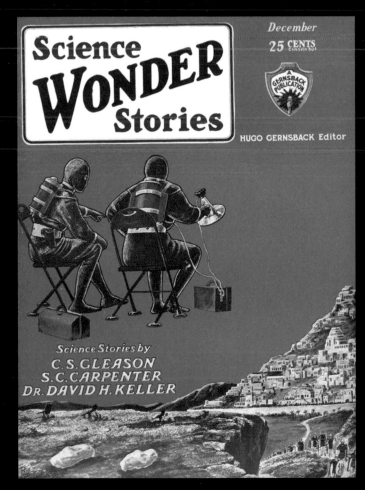

DECEMBER
1929

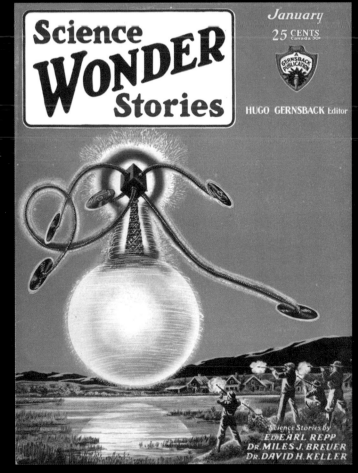

JANUARY
1930

FEBRUARY
1930

MARCH
1930

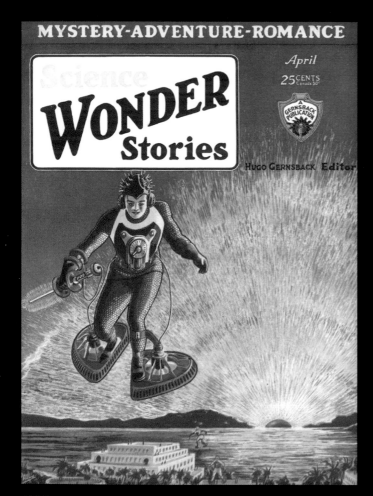

APRIL
1930

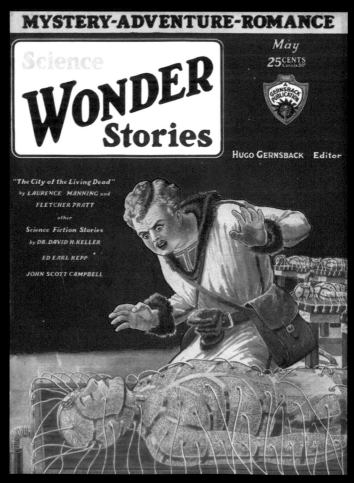

MAY
1930

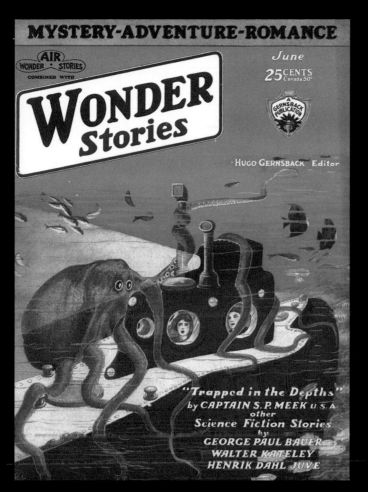

JUNE
1930

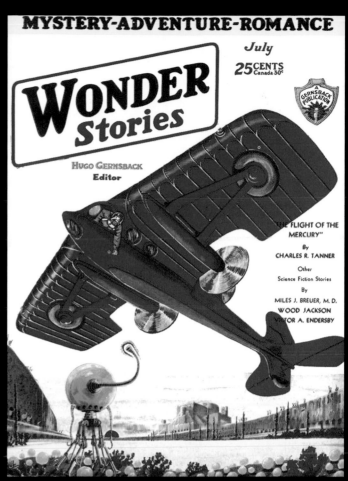

JULY
1930

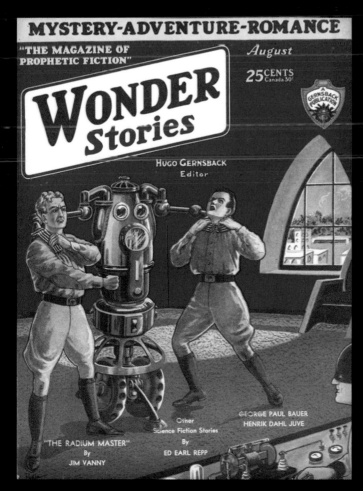

AUGUST
1930

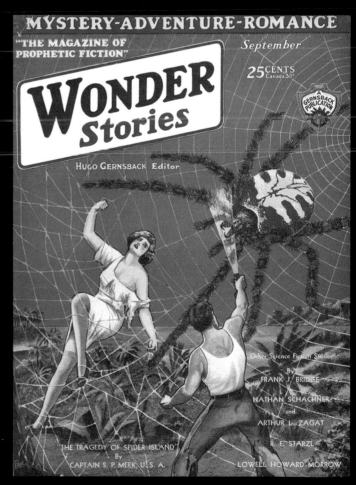

SEPTEMBER
1930

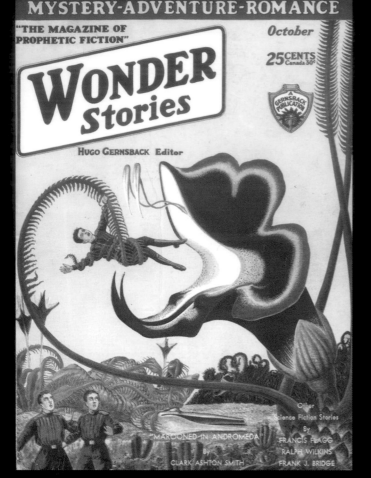

MYSTERY-ADVENTURE-ROMANCE

"THE MAGAZINE OF PROPHETIC FICTION"

October

25 CENTS Canada 30¢

WONDER Stories

HUGO GERNSBACK Editor

Other Science Fiction Stories
In This Issue
By
"MAROONED IN ANDROMEDA" FRANCIS FLAGG
By RALPH WILKINS
CLARK ASHTON SMITH FRANK J. BRIDGE

OCTOBER
1930

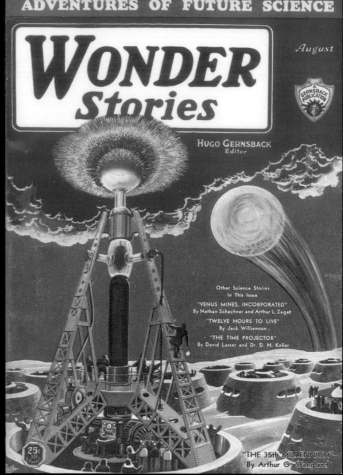

ADVENTURES OF FUTURE SCIENCE

August

WONDER Stories

HUGO GERNSBACK Editor

Other Science Stories
In This Issue
"VENUS MINES, INCORPORATED"
By Nathan Schachner and Arthur L. Zagat
"TWELVE HOURS TO LIVE"
By Jack Williamson
"THE TIME PROJECTOR"
By David Lasser and Dr. D. H. Keller

"THE 35th MILLENNIUM"
By Arthur G. Stangland

AUGUST
1931

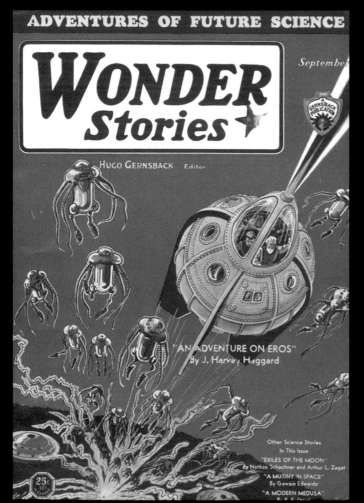

ADVENTURES OF FUTURE SCIENCE

September

WONDER Stories

HUGO GERNSBACK Editor

"AN ADVENTURE ON EROS"
By J. Harvey Haggard

Other Science Stories
In This Issue
"EXILES OF THE MOON"
By Nathan Schachner and Arthur L. Zagat
"A MUTINY IN SPACE"
By Gawain Edwards
"A MODERN MEDUSA"

SEPTEMBER
1931

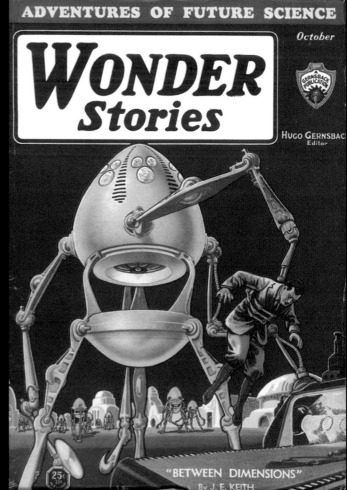

ADVENTURES OF FUTURE SCIENCE

October

WONDER Stories

HUGO GERNSBACK Editor

"BETWEEN DIMENSIONS"
By J. E. KEITH

OCTOBER
1931

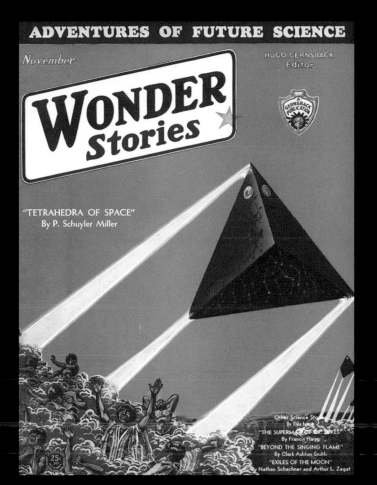

NOVEMBER
1931

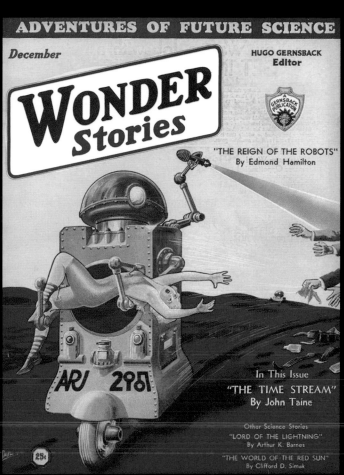

DECEMBER
1931

JANUARY
1932

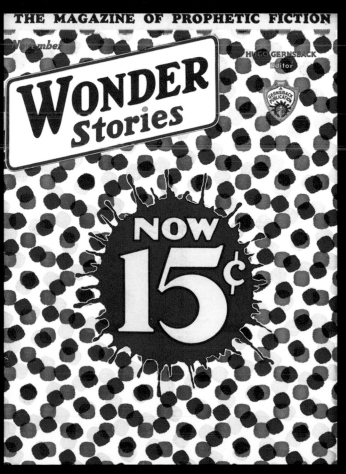

NOVEMBER
1932

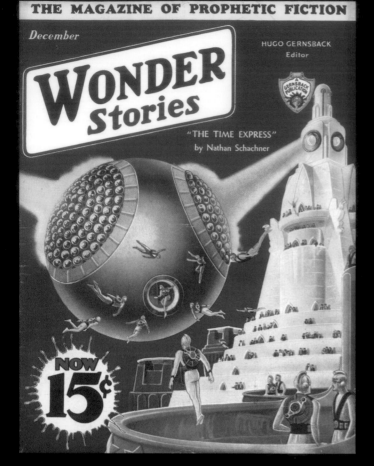

THE MAGAZINE OF PROPHETIC FICTION

DECEMBER
1932

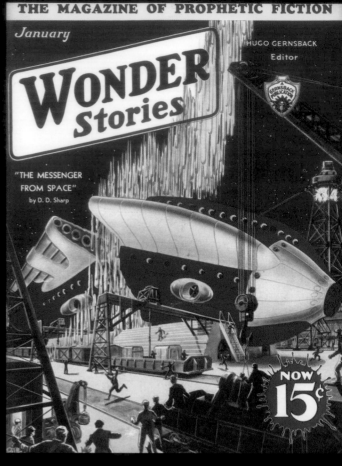

THE MAGAZINE OF PROPHETIC FICTION

JANUARY
1933

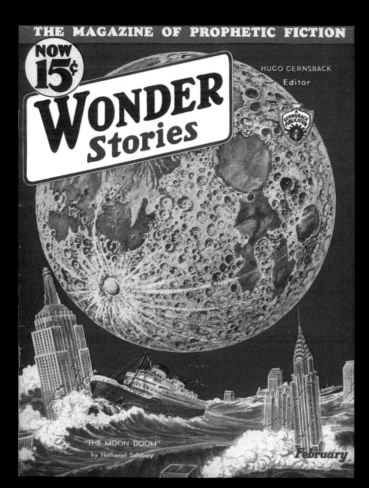

THE MAGAZINE OF PROPHETIC FICTION

FEBRUARY
1933

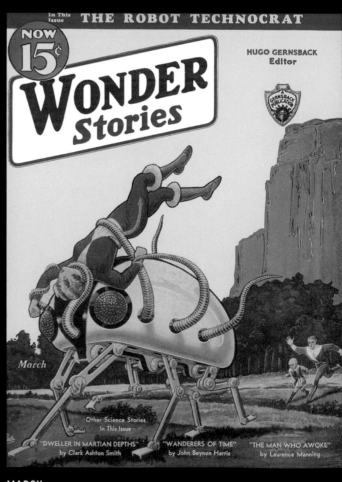

THE ROBOT TECHNOCRAT

MARCH
1933

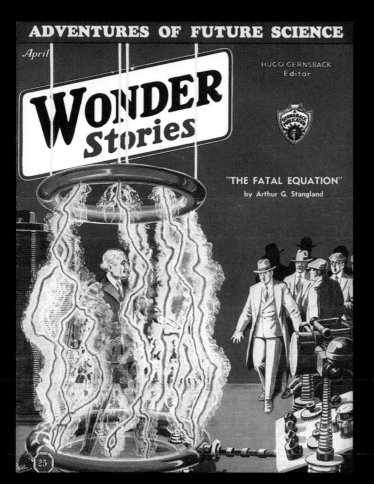

**APRIL
1933**

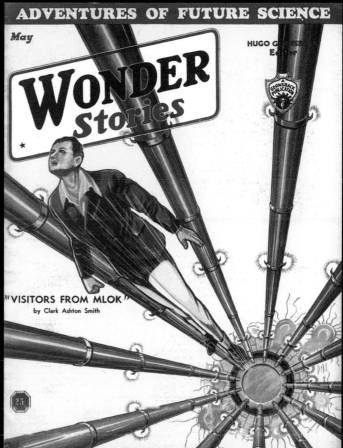

**MAY
1933**

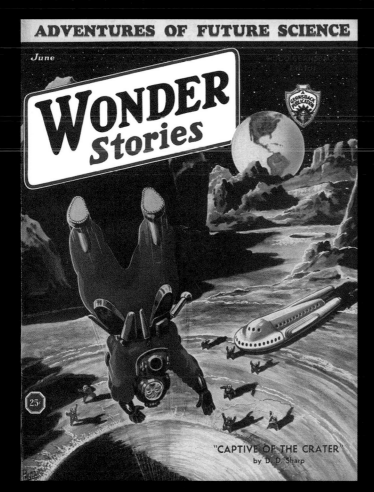

**JUNE
1933**

**AUGUST
1933**

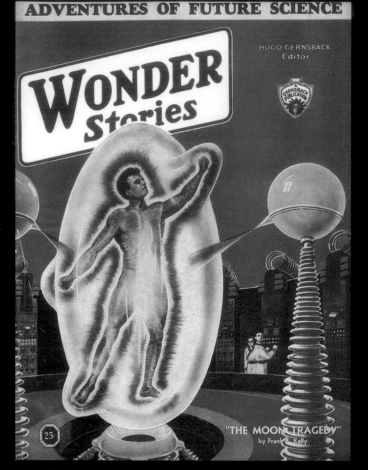

ADVENTURES OF FUTURE SCIENCE

WONDER Stories

HUGO GERNSBACK Editor

"THE MOON TRAGEDY"
by Frank K. Kelly

OCTOBER
1933

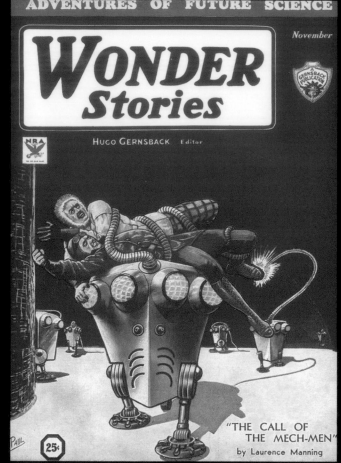

ADVENTURES OF FUTURE SCIENCE

November

WONDER Stories

HUGO GERNSBACK Editor

"THE CALL OF
THE MECH-MEN"
by Laurence Manning

NOVEMBER
1933

ADVENTURES OF FUTURE SCIENCE

December

WONDER Stories

HUGO GERNSBACK Editor

"EVOLUTION SATELLITE"
by J. Harvey Haggard

DECEMBER
1933

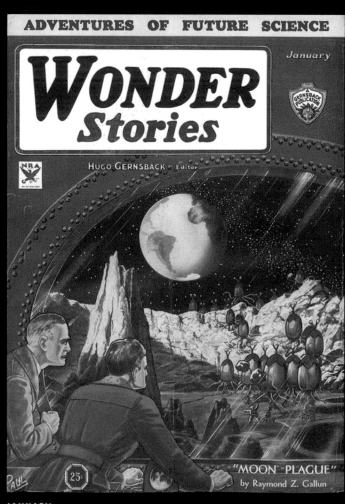

ADVENTURES OF FUTURE SCIENCE

January

WONDER Stories

HUGO GERNSBACK Editor

"MOON PLAGUE"
by Raymond Z. Gallun

JANUARY
1934

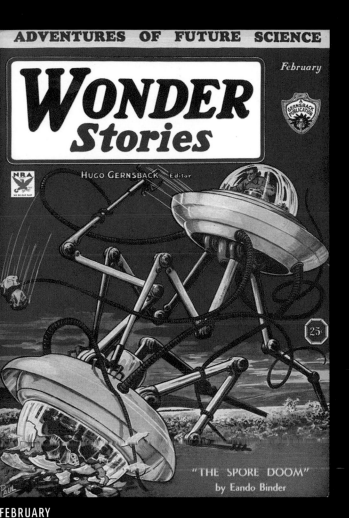

ADVENTURES OF FUTURE SCIENCE

February

WONDER Stories

Hugo Gernsback Editor

"THE SPORE DOOM"
by Eando Binder

FEBRUARY
1934

ADVENTURES OF FUTURE SCIENCE

March

WONDER Stories

Hugo Gernsback Editor

"CHILDREN OF THE RAY"
by J. Harvey Haggard

MARCH
1934

THE BEST IN SCIENCE FICTION

WONDER Stories

"THE MOON DEVILS"
by John Beynon Harris

APRIL

THE BEST IN SCIENCE FICTION

May

WONDER Stories

Hugo Gernsback Editor

SCIENCE FICTION LEAGUE

SEE PAGE 1061

"EARTHSPOT"
By Morrison Colladay

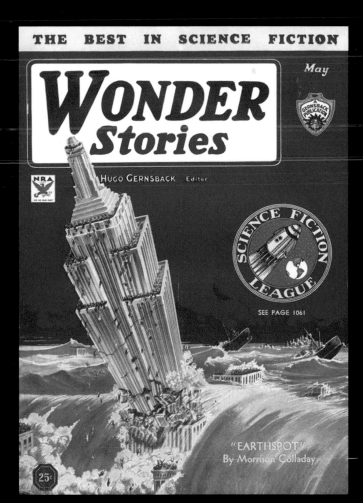

MAY

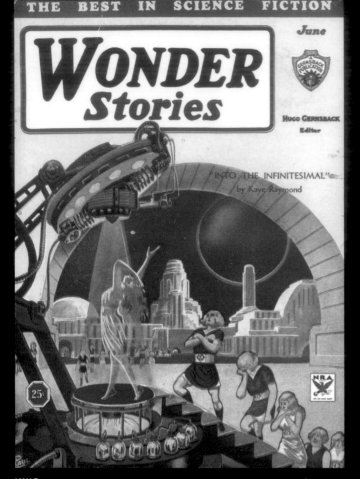

JUNE
1934

JULY
1934

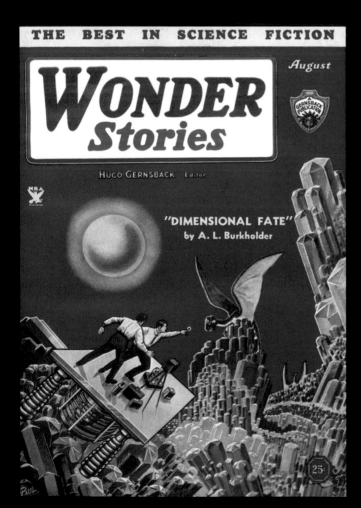

AUGUST
1934

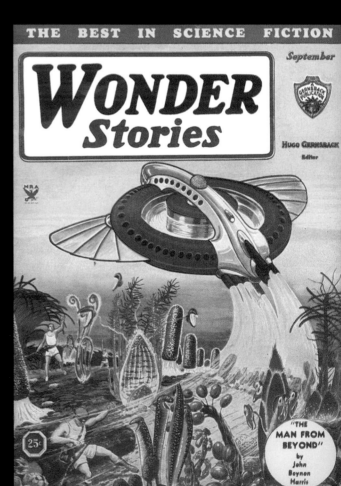

SEPTEMBER
1934

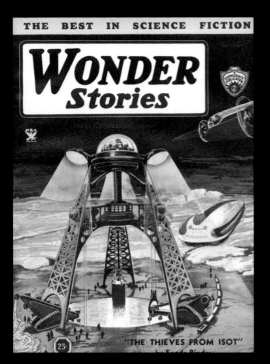

THE BEST IN SCIENCE FICTION

WONDER Stories

"THE THIEVES FROM ISOT"

OCTOBER
1934

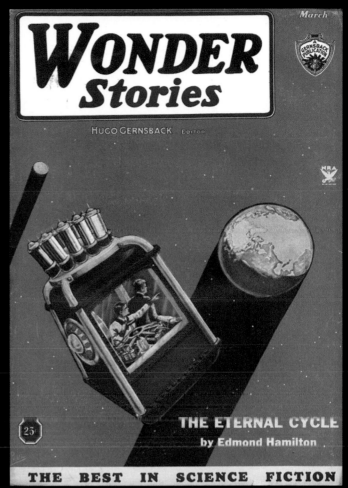

WONDER Stories

HUGO GERNSBACK Editor

THE ETERNAL CYCLE
by Edmond Hamilton

THE BEST IN SCIENCE FICTION

MARCH
1935

WONDER Stories

HUGO GERNSBACK Editor

"ONE WAY TUNNEL"
by David H. Keller, M.D.

JANUARY
1935

THE BEST IN SCIENCE FICTION

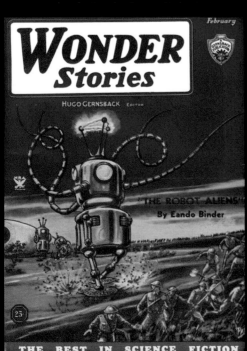

WONDER Stories

HUGO GERNSBACK Editor

THE ROBOT ALIENS
By Eando Binder

FEBRUARY
1935

THE BEST IN SCIENCE FICTION

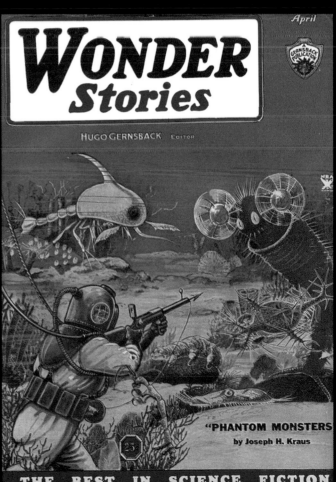

WONDER Stories

HUGO GERNSBACK Editor

"PHANTOM MONSTERS"
by Joseph H. Kraus

APRIL
1935

THE BEST IN SCIENCE FICTION

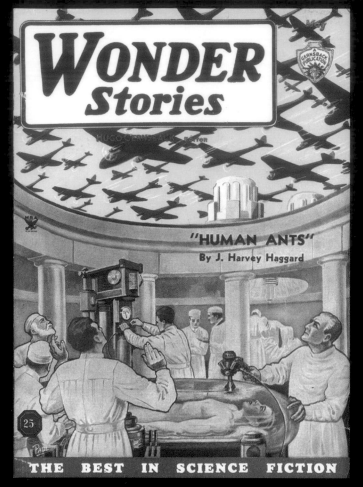

"HUMAN ANTS"
By J. Harvey Haggard

THE BEST IN SCIENCE FICTION

MAY
1935

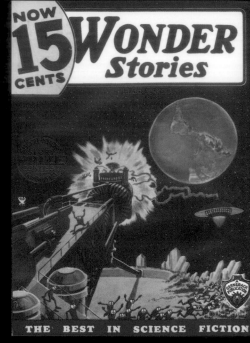

JULY
1935

THE BEST IN SCIENCE FICTION

JUNE
1935

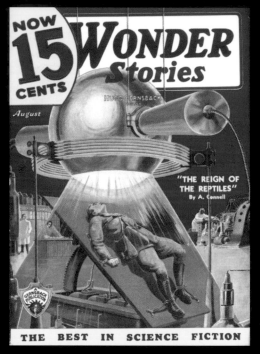

"THE REIGN OF THE REPTILES"
By A. Connell

THE BEST IN SCIENCE FICTION

AUGUST
1935

"THE IDEAL"
by Stanley G. Weinbaum

THE BEST IN SCIENCE FICTION

SEPTEMBER
1935

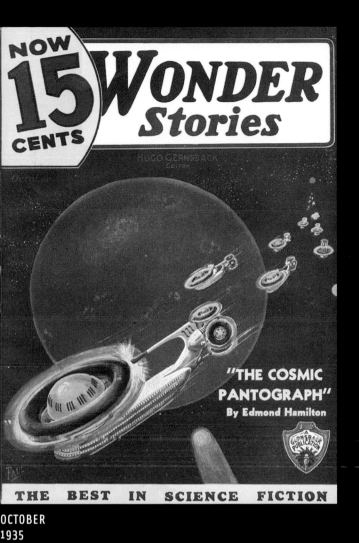

"THE COSMIC PANTOGRAPH"
By Edmond Hamilton

THE BEST IN SCIENCE FICTION

OCTOBER
1935

"DREAM'S END"
By A. Connell

THE BEST IN IMAGINATIVE FICTION

DECEMBER
1935

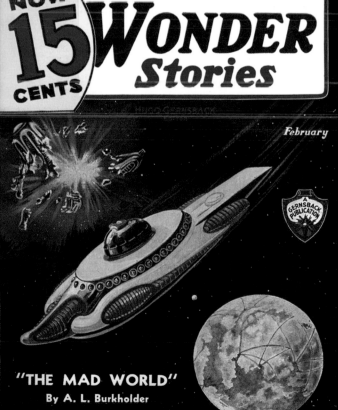

February

"THE MAD WORLD"
By A. L. Burkholder

THE BEST IN IMAGINATIVE FICTION

FEBRUARY
1936

April

NOW 15¢

THE WORLD OF SINGING CRYSTALS
By Thos. S. Gardner

THE BEST IN IMAGINATIVE FICTION

APRIL
1936

JANUARY 20c

COMET

STORIES OF SUPER TIME AND SPACE

On tour with the
Legion of Space
in the
LIGHTNING'S COURSE
by John Victor Peterson

— STF —

Stories by:
HARL VINCENT

— STF —

R. R. WINTERBOTHAM

— STF —

FRANK B. LONG

— STF —

EANDO BINDER

— STF —

FRANK EDWARD
ARNOLD

— STF —

H. L. NICHOLS

— STF —

SAM MOSKOWITZ

— STF —

Don't Miss the
SHORT SHORT
STORY DEPARTMENT
It's Your Opportunity

— STF —

EDITED BY
ORLIN TREMAINE

JANUARY
1941

MAY 1941 20c

COMET

STORIES OF SUPER TIME AND SPACE

Locked in Ice
Caverns on Neptune
in
ICE PLANET
by Carl Selwyn

— STF —

DERELICTS OF URANUS
by J. Harvey Haggard

— STF —

THE FACTS OF LIFE
by P. Schuyler Miller

— STF —

SKY TRAP
by Frank Belknap Long

— STF —

WE ARE ONE
by Eando Binder

— STF —

WHEN TIME ROLLED
BACK
by Ed Earl Repp

— STF —

EDITED BY
ORLIN TREMAINE

MAY
1941

15c
DYNAMIC
SCIENCE STORIES

LORD of TRANERICA
complete novel by
STANTON COBLENTZ

FEB.

MUTINEERS of SPACE
novelet by
LLOYD ESHBACK

PLUS OTHER
GREAT
STORIES

FEBRUARY
1938

NORRIS TAPLEY'S SIXTH SENSE by ED EARL REPP

fantastic
ADVENTURES

APRIL
20c

SEE
BACK
COVER

The BLUE
TROPICS
ADVENTURE IN A WORLD
BENEATH ANTARCTICA
by JAMES NORMAN

AND STORIES BY
NELSON S. BOND   ROBERT BLOCH
JOHN YORK CABOT

APRIL
1940

APRIL
1940

MAY–JUNE
1940

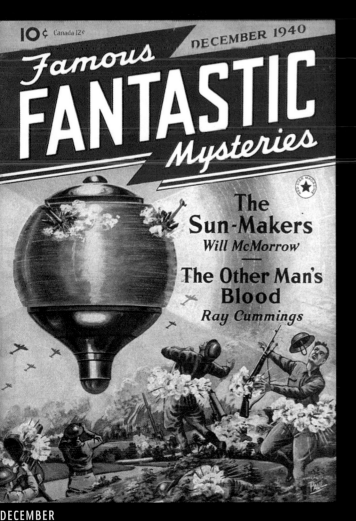

DECEMBER
1940

NOVEMBER
1940

APRIL
1941

FEBRUARY
1938

NOVEMBER
1938

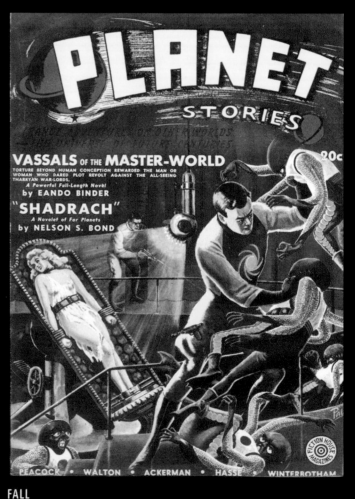

FALL
1941

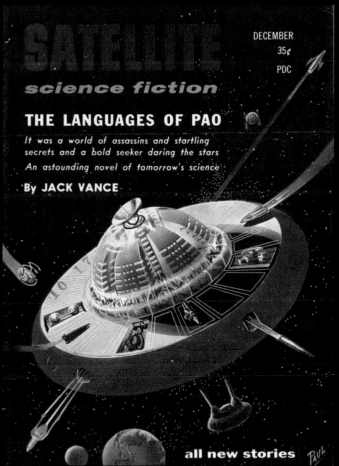

DECEMBER
1957

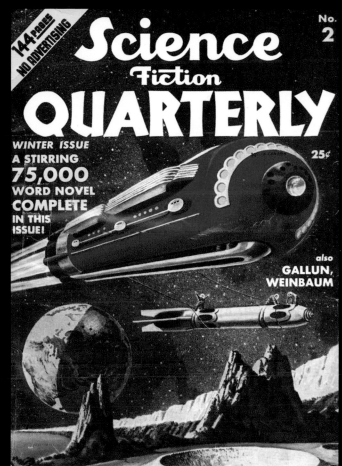

WINTER
1941

SPRING
1941

SUMMER
1941

FRANK R. PAUL ORIGINAL ART

By STEPHEN D. KORSHAK
Captions by JERRY WEIST

Most Frank R. Paul illustration art was not saved and has disappeared. The majority of that art which is still known to exist has been carefully preserved by several collectors. This section displays some highlights from the original art held in those collections.

Opposite: *Frank R. Paul*, February 1933 WONDER STORIES cover entitled "When Worlds Collide" by Philip Wylie and Edwin Balmer. This Illustration was also used for the 1979 edition of *The Science-Fiction Encyclopedia*, edited by Peter Nicholls. From the Korshak collection.

Above: *Frank R. Paul*, original artwork for the painting entitled "Life on Neptune," from the back cover of FANTASTIC ADVENTURES, March 1940, Ziff Davis Publications. From the Korshak collection.

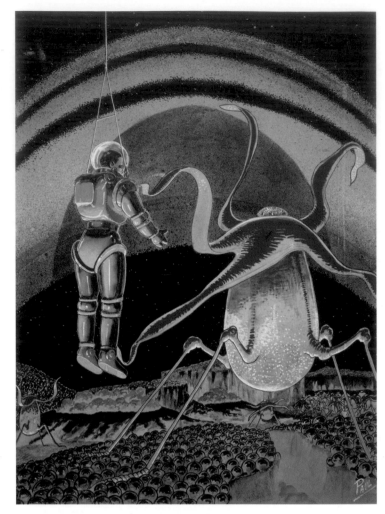

Opposite, top left: *Frank R. Paul,* cover design for the cover to WONDER STORIES, November 1930. From the collection of Robert Weinberg.

Opposite, bottom left: *Frank R. Paul,* cover design for the cover to WONDER STORIES, March of 1935, from "The Eternal Cycle" by Edmond Hamilton. From the Korshak collection.

Opposite, top right: *Frank R. Paul,* cover design for the Back cover to FANTASTIC ADVENTURES, November 1939, entitled "Life On Saturn." From the collection of Howard and Jane Frank

Opposite, bottom right: *Frank R. Paul,* cover design for WONDER STORIES, July 1935. From the collection of Doug and Deb Ellis.

Above: *Frank R. Paul,* original painting for back cover to AMAZING STORIES, December 1941, entitled "Serenis, Water City of Callisto." From the collection of Doug and Deb Ellis.

Opposite: *Frank R. Paul*, original painting for the back cover to AMAZING STORIES, September 1940, entitled "Life on Europa (Moon of Jupiter)." Gouache on board, signed on the lower left. The back cover paintings offered Paul an opportunity to pursue themes based on "Life on Other Worlds." He was also free to design and develop paintings that did not have the dead space usually reserved for the title logo. From the collection of Jerry Weist.

Above: *Frank R. Paul*, original painting for the cover to SCIENCE WONDER STORIES, September 1929 (one of four known to exist from this year), entitled "The Onslaught from Venus," by Frank Phillips. From the collection of Jerry Weist.

Above: *Frank R. Paul,* original painting for the cover to FUTURE FICTION, November 1940. From the collection of Howard and Jane Frank.

Opposite: *Frank R. Paul,* original painting for the cover to WONDER STORIES QUARTERLY, Fall 1931, Volume 3, No. 1. Gouache on board, signed by the artist on the lower left. One of the most dramatic and scientifically realistic covers that Paul did early in his career. From the collection of Jerry Weist.

Opposite: *Frank R. Paul*, interior color painting from SCIENCE FICTION PLUS, June 1953, from the cover theme article entitled "Saturn, Queen of the Sky." Pen and ink with watercolor and gouache with brush on board, signed lower right. From the collection of Jerry Weist

Above: *Frank R. Paul*, original painting for the back cover of an unidentified issue of FANTASTIC ADVENTURES or AMAZING STORIES. From the collection of Robert Lesser.

Right: *Frank R. Paul*, original painting for the cover of WONDER STORIES, September 1935. Gouache on canvas illustration board, signed on the lower left. An early "nightmare" robot theme. From the Collection of Sam Moskowitz.

Bottom left: *Frank R. Paul*, original painting for the cover of AIR WONDER STORIES, December 1929, Vol. 1, No. 6. Gouache on board, signed on the lower left. From the Collection of Jim Halperin.

Bottom right: *Frank R. Paul*, original painting for the cover of WONDER STORIES QUARTERLY, Fall 1929, Vol. 1 No. 1. Gouache on board, signed on the lower left. This is the only surviving Gernsback No. 1 Paul cover. From the Collection of Glynn Crain.

Opposite: *Frank R. Paul*, original painting for the cover of SCIENCE-FICTION PLUS, December 1953. Gouache on board, signed on the lower right. This was the final issue for SF +, and would be Paul's last cover for a Gernsback publication. He did only two more science-fiction covers; for the 35th Anniversary AMAZING STORIES issue, and the December 1957 cover for SATELLITE SCIENCE FICTION. From the Collection of Jerry Weist.

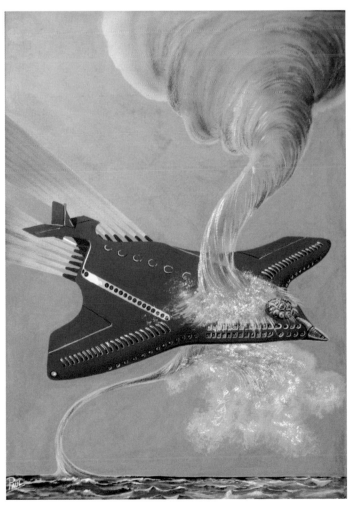

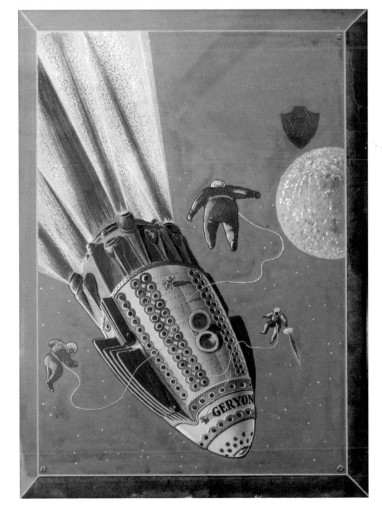

Above: *Frank R. Paul*, painting for WONDER STORIES, Vol. 5, No. 2, August 1933, for J. Harvey Haggard's "Castaways on Deimos." Gouache on illustration board, signed on the lower left. From the collection of Glynn Crain.

Opposite: *Frank R. Paul*, painting for AIR WONDER STORIES, August 1929, Vol. 1, No. 2, for Henrik Dahl Juve's "The Silent Destroyer," (one of only four paintings surviving from that year). Gouache on illustration board, signed by the artist on the lower left. This is one of the finest early surviving Paul paintings with its prophetic visual image that brings to mind the Hindenburg disaster over New Jersey on May 6, 1937–fully eight years before the first great airborne disaster took place. From the collection of Glynn Crain.

Frank R. Paul, painting for SCIENCE WONDER QUARTERLY, Winter 1930, Vol. 1, No. 2, illustrating a scene from R.H. Romans "The Moon Conquerors." Gouache on illustration board, signed on the lower right. This painting was originally from the collection of Sam Moskowitz, and was sold as the cover lot for Sotheby's 1999 Sam Moskowitz Science Fiction Collection. From the collection of Glynn Crain.

Frank R. Paul, painting for WONDER STORIES QUARTERLY, Spring 1932, Vol. 3, No. 3, from J.M. Wash's "The Vanguard to Neptune." Gouache on illustration board, signed on the lower left. From the collection of Glynn Crain.

Frank R. Paul, double page illustration from ASTONISHING STORIES, February 1943, for Robert Bloch's "It Happened Tomorrow." Pen and ink with brush on paper, signed. From the collection of Jerry Weist.

Above: *Frank R. Paul*, back cover painting for
AMAZING STORIES, 1941. Gouache on board, signed
lower left. From the collection of Robert Lesser.

Opposite: *Frank R. Paul*, cover painting for WONDER
STORIES QUARTERLY, Spring 1931. Gouache on board,
signed lower left. From the collection of Robert Lesser.

PAUL

GERNSBACK FLAME TANK 1935

Above left: *Frank R. Paul,* cover painting for EVERYDAY SCIENCE AND MECHANICS, January 1936. From the Howard and Jane Frank collection.

Left: *Frank R. Paul,* cover painting for SCIENCE FICTION, October 1940. From the Howard and Jane Frank collection.

Above: *Frank R. Paul,* cover painting for SCIENCE FICTION, December 1939. Gouache on board, signed lower right. From the collection of Robert Lesser.

Opposite: *Frank R. Paul,* painting for the cover of SCIENCE FICTION QUARTERLY, Winter 1941. Oil on canvas, signed lower left. From a private collection.

118

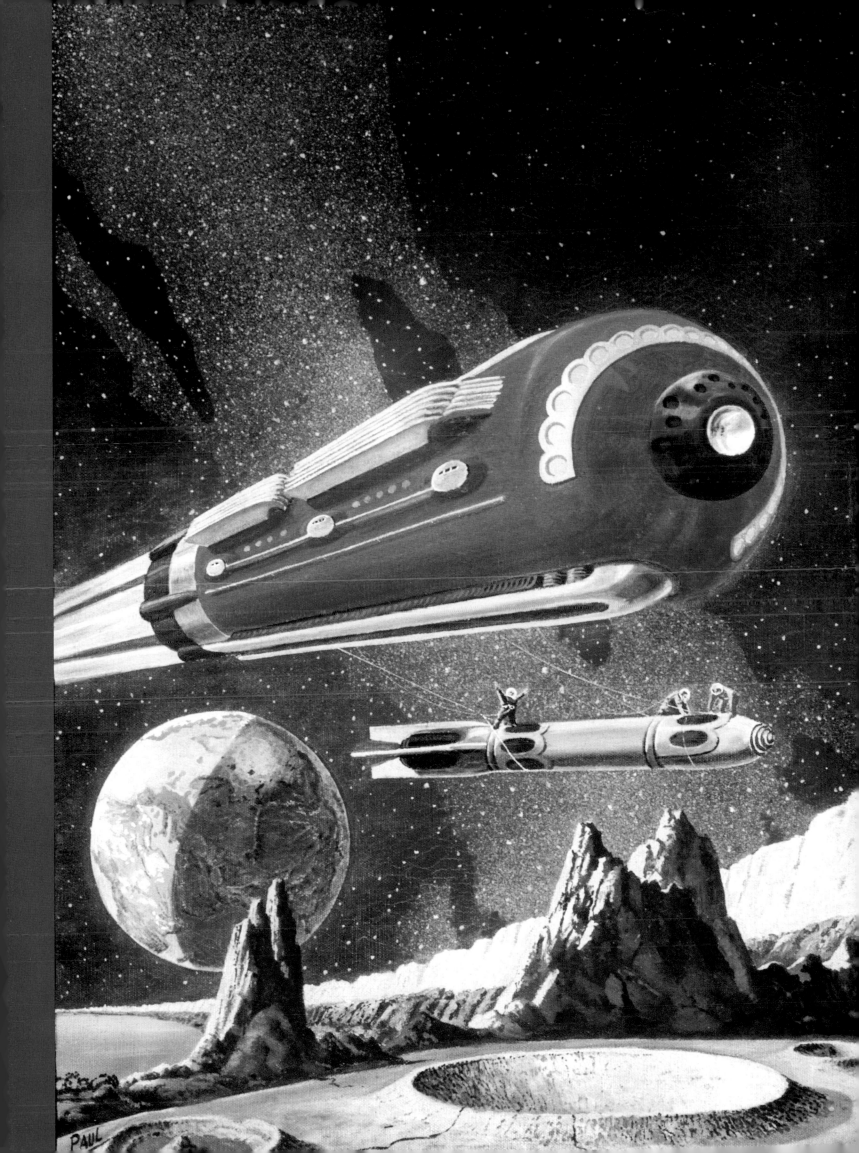

Opposite, top left: *Frank R. Paul*, original painting for the cover to WONDER STORIES, November 1931, Vol. 3, No. 6. from P. Schuyler Miller's "Tetrahedra of Space." From the collection of Jerry Weist.

Opposite, top right: *Frank R. Paul*, original painting for the cover to WONDER STORIES, August 1930, Vol. 2, No. 3, for Jim Vanny's "The Radium Master." Gouache on board, signed lower left. From the collection of Jerry Weist.

Opposite, bottom left: *Frank R. Paul*, back cover painting for an unidentified AMAZING STORIES QUARTERLY, 1940s. Gouache on board, signed lower left. From the collection of Jerry Weist

Opposite, bottom right: *Frank R. Paul*, cover painting for WONDER STORIES, August 1934. Gouache on board, signed. From the collection of Robert Lesser.

Right: *Frank R. Paul*, original painting for the cover to WONDER STORIES, May 1933, Vol. 4, No. 12, from Clark Ashton Smith's story "Visitors from Mlok." Gouache on board, signed on the lower left. From the Collection of Jerry Weist.

Above: *Frank R. Paul*, front cover painting for FANTASTIC ADVENTURES, April 1940, entitled "The Blue Tropics." Gouache on board, signed lower right. From the Korshak collection.

Opposite: *Frank R. Paul*, original painting for the back cover of FANTASTIC ADVENTURES, July 1939, Vol. 1, No. 2, entitled "The Man From Venus." Gouache on board, signed lower right. From the collection of Eric Gewirz.

AFTERWORD:
A BRUSH WITH GENIUS

by

FORREST J ACKERMAN

Frank Rudolph Paul, it could truly be said, was Austria's gift to the wonderful realm of science-fiction art. From his first cover on the world's first science-fiction magazine, *Amazing Stories* for April 1926, and for the next 30 years, his beatific brushes (of which I am thrilled to own three) and enchanted palette graced the covers and interiors of the sci-fi pulps.

I wasted the first nine years of my life but in October 1926, was standing in front of a magazine rack with mundane magazines of the time such as *Delineator, Ladies Home Journal, Red Book,* et.al., and suddenly I was mesmerized by that month's *Amazing Stories* with a Paul cover for Part 2 of "Beyond the Pole" by A. Hyatt Verrill. The magazine then JUMPED off the rack, grabbed hold of me, and (magazines spoke in those days) cried, "Take me home, Little Boy, you will love me!"

Needless to add, Frank Rudolph Paul and his fabulous sci-fi artwork brought me into what became my lifetime advocation and vocation.

Forrest J Ackerman, agent, editor, author, actor, collector and legendary fan was affectionately known as "Mr. Science Fiction."

Above: Forrest J Ackerman at the Ackermansion in front of the illustration on page 124, the second commissioned "gold" painting from Frank R. Paul, which was finished in 1960. Photo courtesy of the collection of Forrest J Ackerman.

Opposite: *Frank R. Paul,* original painting commissioned by Forrest J Ackerman in the 1950s, based on a cover for Hugo Gernsback's SCIENCE AND INVENTION. Gouache with gold-leaf background and brush on board, signed lower left. This was the second and final commission from Ackerman to Paul. Originally from the collection of Forrest J Ackerman, now in a private collection.

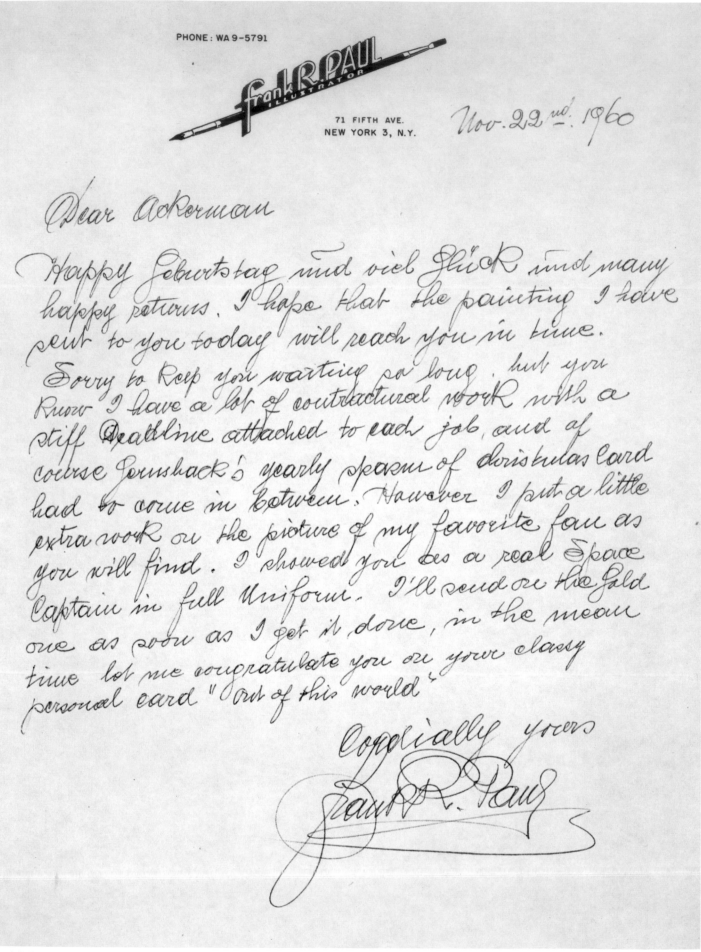

71 FIFTH AVE.
NEW YORK 3, N.Y.

Nov. 22nd. 1960

Dear Ackerman

Happy Geburtstag und viel Glück und many happy returns. I hope that the painting I have sent to you today will reach you in time.

Sorry to keep you waiting so long, but you know I have a lot of contractual work with a stiff deadline attached to each job, and of course Gernsback's yearly spasm of christmas card had to come in between. However I put a little extra work on the picture of my favorite fan as you will find. I showed you as a real Space Captain in full uniform. I'll send on the fold one as soon as I get it done, in the mean time let me congratulate you on your classy personal card "Out of this world"

Cordially yours

Frank R. Paul

Frank R. Paul, personal letter to Forrest J Ackerman, with descriptions for his finishing of the two consigned paintings by Ackerman in 1960.